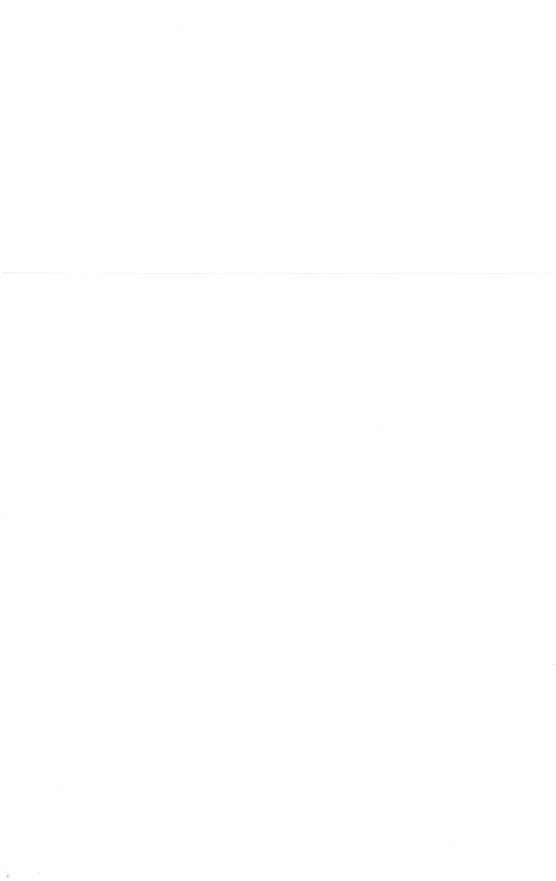

YOU
ARE THE BRAND,
STUPID!

How To *Get Noticed,*
Gain Instant Credibility,
Make Millions and
Dominate Your Competition
By Building Your
Expert Brand

TRACY E. MYERS, CMD
WITH BRUCE ROFFEY

WEP
WORLDWIDE EXPERT PRESS

Contents

Introduction:
Why You Are the Brand, Stupid!

If you are in business—whether you're the boss or you work for a corporation—there's something important you need to know.

In today's fast-paced world, people make decisions very quickly. That means—if you want people to employ you or buy your products and services—they first of all need to have heard of you, and then they need a good reason to choose you.

Becoming a celebrity in your market

The first step in that process is becoming well-known.

The fact is we live in a world today where people are obsessed with celebrity. The people who sell the most records are not always the best singers or musicians, and the biggest box office stars are not always the best actors.

Those who get to the top understand the power of celebrity, and they work hard at building their image and reputation so that they stay at the top.

It's a lesson that has been learned by top politicians and business leaders—if you want to be president of the United States, you had better write a book or two first. If you want to be a business power broker, a TV show will help.

But the power of celebrity is not only relevant to stars and big corporations. The exact same techniques can be used in any line of business—whether you work on your own, run a business, or work for someone else. I've seen that work for real in my own life and time, and again, I've seen it transform the results of my most successful clients.

In this book, I'm going to share some stories of how the power of celebrity can help take your business or career to new levels of success. And I'm going to reveal some of the exact techniques you can use to make it start happening today.

Becoming the recognized expert in your market

However, let's be clear; the power of celebrity alone is not enough to make your business or career deliver its full potential. You need substance not just glamour!

That means you don't just want to be a celebrity. You want to position yourself as an INDUSTRY EXPERT and be a TRUSTED ADVISOR.

In order to achieve that, you need to define your market clearly and establish genuine reasons why you should be the choice in that market. You need to build a brand that positions you as the go-to expert in your field.

Now, you may think that brands are only for big businesses with huge advertising budgets. But the fact is that all businesses have a brand—it's simply the way people perceive them.

It's the same for you as an individual. You have a brand whether you want one or not. So why not make the effort to develop the right brand? I'm going to show you exactly how to create a powerful brand that makes you the obvious choice in a profitable market.

Becoming the industry expert in your market

You know, there really is something special about you—a reason why people should choose you over the competition. You may just need to work out exactly what that is.

However, if you follow the right process, you can easily be the "go-to" expert in your field. It's simply a matter of making sure you define the right field of expertise, and then take the steps needed to establish your expert status.

So, in this book, I'll also set out how you can define your market properly and become clear about your expert status. Then I'll share the techniques you can use to make sure your expertise is known to the right people.

I know the idea of becoming a local celebrity by positioning yourself as an industry expert can seem intimidating to many people. But it's simply the fastest, best, and easiest way of creating a successful, highly profitable business or career in any field.

If you follow the right process.

So, in this book, I'll set out the step-by-step process you need to follow to make sure you choose the right market, establish a great expert brand, and promote it to attract your ideal customers easily.

Remember, as an industry expert, you're not just getting publicity. You're establishing yourself as the first choice among your ideal customers (or employers). That's the *real* route to success.

Here are the steps we'll follow:

1. Harnessing the Power of Personality for Your Brand

2. Matching Your Expertise to Your Perfect Market

3. Defining Your Expert Brand

4. 10 Proven Strategies for Building a Winning Expert Brand

5. Creating and Using Your Personal Story To Establish Yourself As An Industry Expert

Now don't worry, you don't have to be an Oprah or a Lady Gaga. This works for everyone—you just need to be yourself.

You may already have taken some of the steps I'll explain here, or you may be starting with a completely blank sheet. Either way, this process will help you build a more satisfying, rewarding, and successful business or career.

It's time to create your own successful expert brand and start living the lifestyle you really want.

CHAPTER 1

Harnessing the Power of Personality for Your Brand

In the rest of this book, I'm going to share the key steps and strategies you need to follow in order to build a powerful expert brand. If you follow these steps, you'll stand out way ahead of your competition.

However, in this section, I want to share one secret that will take you to a completely new level. That secret is the power of your own personality.

Overcoming the dull, corporate approach

Every day in my work, I meet people who have amazing personalities. Then I go and check out their blogs, their articles, videos, and books—any of the ways they represent themselves in their business world. I often discover that they are totally flat and stale—they have a dull, corporate feeling.

I have to tell you that if you truly want to establish yourself as the go-to expert in your market, you have to do the exact opposite. This dull, corporate approach is *not* what your clients and prospects want. They want to know who you really are.

The fact is that we connect best with people we can relate to; who are like us in some way—whether it's the way they think, their lifestyle, their age, their background … whatever.

So, if you want to build your expert brand, your expertise has to align with your personality and who you're trying to connect with. This may seem scary at first, but you have to let people in on who you truly are.

You've probably heard it said that success is 10 percent what you know and 90 percent the rest. I'm not sure if these numbers are correct, but I am sure the message is spot-on. In short, people have to know you before they'll listen to you. If they don't know who you are, then they don't know if they should take your advice. So, you've got to let them in.

And yes, that does mean you need to show them your quirks and idiosyncrasies.

Now, there may be things you don't want to get into—such as politics and religion—but you should be aware that the more polarizing you are, the more magnetic you will become to those who are like you.

Polarizing for success

The more you let people know who you really are, the more they'll either see themselves in you or they'll see they're not like you.

So, it's also true that the more polarizing you are, the more you'll push some people away. But the benefit of that is that the people who identify with you will be even more attracted to you.

You can probably think of personalities right now—whether in business or in entertainment—that you cannot stand. You just can't figure out how they have such a big following. Well, it's because of this rule. There are people who feel like them, and the more polarizing they are, the more they're drawn to them.

I'm going to show you exactly how to position yourself so that the right potential customers are attracted to you. But let me start by sharing a little of me and how I came to write this book.

My Personal Branding Story Part I

My story dates back more than 82 years—and no, I'm not that old! That's when my great-grandfather opened the first Frank Myers store. And, to most people, it seemed obvious that I would follow in the family of being a small business owner and an entrepreneur.

However, I had other plans. I wanted no part of the family business. I wanted to be in the entertainment industry. From the age of 5 or 6, I only wanted to be a rock star, radio DJ, or an actor.

I guess that's not too unusual for a 5-year-old, but I actually started to live my dream pretty quickly. When I was 8, my brother and I got a couple of the neighborhood kids together to put on a play in my backyard. We practiced every day for two weeks after school.

I made posters by hand advertising the play—remember, this was before PCs and there was no Kinko's. We made copies using carbon paper and put them in the neighbors' mailboxes.

We didn't charge admission, but I DID pass the plate. We may not have had an audience of thousands, but I did manage to get $55 in donations—that's not too bad when you're only 8.

I gave my two friends and my brother $5 each, which left me a hefty profit of $40.

So, I was lucky enough to learn three very important lessons early on in life:

> *I loved being on a stage in front of people. I loved the applause, the accolades, and the CELEBRITY! (The money wasn't bad either!)*

> *Marketing something—in fact, anything—came naturally to me.*

> *If you were creative and didn't mind a little hard work, you didn't have to spend a lot of money marketing to get great results.*

In the rest of this book, I'm going to share a few more lessons that I've learned. I'll also tell you a bit more about how the story developed in the following years. But right now, let's get started on thinking about your brand.

CHAPTER 2

Matching Your Expertise to Your Perfect Market

I know you want to get straight in to the exciting, fun parts of building an expert brand. And, don't worry, that's not too far away. But time and again, I've seen people making the big mistake of rushing in without thinking through the important steps of defining a clear market and understanding how their own expertise fits with that market.

Missing out these steps means they end up being an expert in something that nobody is really interested in. Or they find they are trying to position themselves in a field where they don't have the credibility required.

I can assure you that taking a bit of time to work through these steps will make the later steps much easier and more rewarding. If you take time to get to know your market, and then make the effort to clearly understand the benefits of what you offer, you can certainly find a market where you become the go to industry expert.

When you reach that stage, you'll find you'll attract the right customers and clients much more easily. Your business and career will grow to new levels of success, and your lifestyle will be transformed.

So, are you ready to position yourself as the industry expert in a highly profitable market?

This part of the process requires three steps:

1. Understanding yourself and your offer

2. Understanding your market and what they want

3. Matching your offer with what your market wants

So let's examine them one at a time.

1. Understanding Yourself and Your Offer

The first step in the process of positioning yourself as an industry expert is getting to know yourself and what makes you special. This is the core around which you will build your business proposition.

Over time, this will evolve and grow as you build your expert brand, but you need some key starting points.

There is a lot of self-reflection in this step, but you'll find it helps to involve others in the process. For example, you can ask people who know you well for their feedback. You may feel that you have particular strengths, but others may notice something else that seems more important. In fact, we often overlook our biggest strengths because they are what come naturally to us. But these can be extremely important as they often reflect what makes us special.

Another way to get help from someone else during the process is to have them ask you some key questions so that you can discuss your answers.

Here are some exercises for you to kick off this process:

> List your strongest skills

> Identify the top reasons people come to you for help and advice rather than go to someone else

> List the key words your friends, colleagues, and clients say about you to others

> Identify at least one thing you do better than most other people

> Identify the top three reasons most of your customers or clients come to you

> Identify at least one thing that makes you different from your main competitors

Treat this process as a brainstorming—don't question your ideas at this stage. Take a note of everything that comes to your mind. Something that may seem quite unimportant to you may be very significant to your potential clients. Remember that it's a great idea to consult with others as part of this process.

2. Understanding Your Market and What They Want

Of course, knowing yourself is only part of the story. It's even more important to get to know your target market. If you don't know who is in your market, you won't be able to reach them, and you won't make money. If you don't know what they want, you'll have no chance of satisfying their needs.

The better you get to know your market, the more chance you will have of becoming special to them and of building a successful business. The first part of this process is to define your ideal customer.

> ➢ Identify the key characteristics of your ideal customer—details such as age, gender, hobbies, geographic location

> ➢ Define the most important psychological factors of your ideal customer—such as what's important to them, what motivates them, what they want to achieve

> ➢ Describe why you like working with your ideal customers

> ➢ Identify where your ideal customers hang out and where you can connect with them—online and off-line

The key to having the right target market is that it should be small enough for you to become recognized as a specialist, but it should be large enough to enable you to make a lot of money.

The next step in understanding your market is being clear about what they are looking for. People always buy something for one of the following reasons:

1. To get pleasure or make their life better in some way

2. To avoid/reduce pain or solve a problem

Most products or services do one or the other—some do both. Ideally, you should be able to present what you do in both categories. The following exercises will help.

> List the biggest problems your target market faces

> Identify why they still haven't solved the problem

> Describe how your product or service makes their life better

As always, it's a good idea to get someone else to give you feedback in this process. You could even ask your customers directly.

The key to promoting your expert brand is ensuring that you talk to your market in terms of benefits. Focus on how what you do makes their life different.

It's crucial to understand the difference between benefits and features. Features are simply the facts about your product or service. Your customers and prospects want to know what you can do for them to make their lives easier, better, more fun, or more profitable. So make sure you take time to identify what your clients are really looking for from your services and present this in the form of benefits.

There is nothing wrong with being able to list features of your product or service, but you need to be able to turn those into something that has a benefit for your customer. The key question is "what does that mean for me?"

Here are some examples:

Feature	Benefit
We Are Open Weekends	You don't have to take time off work
500 Branches	We have an outlet near you
Highly Trained Staff	We can advise on the best choice for your needs

> ➢ List all the benefits your service offers your customers. Then be ready to use these benefits in all your communication with customers and prospects.

3. Matching Your Offer with What the Market Wants

So, now you have taken time to understand what makes you special and to define exactly what the market is looking for. The next step is to match these together to ensure you present your strengths in a way that meets the needs of your market.

The benefit you are offering to your market must outweigh the cost to them—whether financial, time, or anything else. If they want the benefit but won't pay the cost, you won't build the business you are hoping for.

For example ...

> ➤ **Would you pay $1,000 to attend a seminar that taught you how to make $1,000?** Probably not—unless it offered significant other benefits—because you are investing time as well as money.

> ➤ **Would you pay $1,000 to attend a seminar that taught you how to earn $100,000?** Possibly—provided you had confidence that it would deliver and it was something that appealed to you.

Building a successful business is as simple as that. You need to give people something they want at a price they see as value-for-money.

Of course, the actual return doesn't have to be monetary. Often people are looking for another type of benefit, but they have to feel the return justifies the investment.

In order to give your expert brand the greatest chance of success, you should ideally be offering a service that not only meets their needs but also provides you with a strong connection, either through specific experience or a particular passion. If you have a strong passion for your market, your customers will notice that and you will be more motivated to do what needs to be done.

If necessary, use this process as a chance to reinvent yourself—to do something a little bit different with your life. It may involve more work for a while, but the results will justify it, both, in your business and your personal happiness.

My Personal Branding Story Part 2

When I was in sixth grade, a lightbulb went off in my head while I was at a school dance. The math teacher was playing DJ, and it was horrible. Everyone was threatening to walk out and not come to the next dance. The problem was the dance was a major school fundraiser—they were charging $5 per student admission, PLUS taking pictures and making money off them too.

I came up with a business plan and presented it to the principal, saying I would DJ the next school dance—all they had to do was raise the ticket price from $5 to $7 and give the extra $2 to me. Two hundred students at $2 each made me $400—plus I charged $1 for each "request" that I played and made an extra $50!

The dance was such a success that the principal practically begged me to DJ the rest of the dances ... the feedback was so huge that even more students came to the next dance ... which meant even more money for me!

And here's the best part—I had become such a celebrity in school that a lot of the girls wanted their pictures taken with ME instead of their dates!

By the time I was in high school, I was DJ'ing a couple of times a month for schools, reunions, Christmas parties … anyone that would pay me. But I was using my home stereo equipment.

So I drew up a business plan for my dad and asked him to borrow $1,500 so I could buy some "real" commercial mobile DJ equipment. He agreed and even drove me to the audio store to help me negotiate the price on the equipment. On the way home, he stopped and ordered me some business cards!

When we got back home, Dad drew up a promissory note and even charged me interest—one of the best lessons he ever taught me!

Once I had my "real" equipment, I started booking more gigs and charging more money. I quickly moved on from the high school dance scene because of the lack of money involved. I moved on to colleges and wedding receptions instead.

In my senior year of high school, I made more than $15,000 as a self-employed part-time DJ!

CHAPTER 3

Defining Your Expert Brand

Now that you've identified what makes you special and got to know what your market is looking for, it's time to start developing your Expert Brand.

When you have a strong Expert Brand, you will stand out from the competition. When people need your product or service, they will quickly see that you are exactly the expert they are looking for to give them what they want.

Your Expert Brand needs to answer the questions that a prospective customer will have in their mind about you. The nineteenth-century English poet Rudyard Kipling had a good way of identifying the key questions you need to ask. He wrote:

> *"I keep six honest serving-men (They taught me all I knew);*
> *Their names are What and Why and When*
> *And How and Where and Who."*

If you can give good answers to these questions about your business, you have the building blocks of a strong Expert Brand.

Here is how we would rephrase the most important of Kipling's questions for your brand:

> ➢ Who are you?

>> ▪ This may be simply your name and an overview of your expertise.

> ➢ What do you do?

>> ▪ This explains what you do for people—always in terms of the results people get when they work with you. Never talk about the process or the job title.

> ➢ How do you do it?

>> ▪ This is where you explain the process of working with people—for example, it may be that you set up an initial meeting or you may arrange weekly coaching sessions over six months.

> ➢ Why should I buy from you?

>> ▪ This is very important—you need to give people specific reasons why you are the right person to meet their needs.

These are the key questions in defining your brand, but the other two questions can be important too.

Answering the question about "when" describes your availability. This is most important if you have some element of exclusivity, such as a waiting list for your services, or they are only available at fixed times, e.g., training courses.

The "where" question is about how people get in touch with you—it may be simply a Web site address, or an office, or it may be the types of places you advertise.

Let's look at an example using a career coach:

Who are you?

I'm Joe Edwards, president of Better Careers Inc. I'm part of a team of 20 career-coaching experts based in San Francisco.

What do you do?

I help people who are stuck in a rut to get their ideal job within three months.

How do you do it?

I help them identify what they really want to do, and then I show them exactly what they need to do to get their dream job—I guide them through every step of the process.

Why should I buy from you?

We are the only firm that gives you guaranteed results within three months or your money back.

When do you do it?

We only work with 100 people at a time, and we have a waiting list of about six weeks, but we can schedule an initial consultation at any time.

Where can I find you?

Visit our Web site or call our office.

This process may seem simple and the explanations short. However, these are important questions that help you clarify who your customers are and how you can help them. Most important, it helps you understand—and explain to your customers—why they should do business with you.

Getting the right answers to these questions can help you define a powerful expert brand. It's important to note that these answers are designed to help you establish whether a potential customer is right for you as much as to persuade them to work with you. If they can relate to the way you are positioning what you do, there may be a great fit.

On the other hand, it helps you avoid wasting time with people who are not looking for what you are offering.

Being able to work with your ideal clients is not only more fun—it will also be more successful. People who are in tune with the way you work will get better results.

My Personal Branding Story Part 3

My best friend Eric helped me DJ quite a bit. We always had stars in our eyes and quickly learned the art of self-promotion. We formed several singing groups and bands over the years, but our first singing group was attempting to capitalize on the big craze of the moment ... boy bands!

Eric & I (along with three of our friends) learned as many New Kids on the Block songs as we could, learned the choreography, and wanted to stage our own concert. So we went to work and "booked" the local community center building on a Saturday night. We borrowed stage risers from our high school, hired a sound and light company, and got our moms to collect money at the door and run concessions.

We even did radio interviews, wrote press releases for the local papers, created our own posters ... WHEW!

Thinking back, it's amazing that we weren't nervous. We were so confident in our self-marketing abilities that we KNEW there would be a full house. And you know what? We were right. The place was PACKED. Being a local celebrity was great. I was learning my craft early in life.

CHAPTER 4

10 Proven Strategies for Building a Winning Expert Brand

So now that you've identified your market and defined your expert brand, it's time to get out there and tell the world about it by building your celebrity status.

You won't get noticed by staying at home or sitting in the office waiting for the world to discover your genius. You need to take action and make sure you keep yourself in front of your ideal audience.

It's not only a good idea to get better known—if you truly believe you can make a difference in people's lives, it's your duty to tell them about it. However, it's not just a matter of rushing out and trying to attract attention. You need to choose the right strategies, make sure they deliver a clear message, and work together as part of an effective plan.

If you want to get known, you need to undertake a range of activities, but you'll find that certain strategies work well for you depending on your message, your skills, your market, and your personality.

TRACY E. MYERS, CMD

Some people thrive on publicity and others love blogging or writing. Events are perfect in some markets, and newsletters make the biggest impact in others. For some businesses, Twitter is the place to be seen; for others, it's a complete waste of time. The secret is to find the mix that is right for you and to develop an effective plan to make them deliver results.

In this section, I'm going to share my 10 favorite techniques for helping anyone define their expert brand and build their celebrity status. (Actually, I've got a few bonus tips thrown in at the end as well.) You don't need to use all of these techniques and strategies from day one. But you've got to get started somewhere, and using even a few of them will help you establish yourself as a celebrity in your market.

Here are the 10 strategies we'll cover in detail.

1. Have a great Web site

2. Create a crowd-pulling blog

3. Generate loads of publicity

4. Publish a newsletter that people want to read

5. Write an expert book

6. Make a "splash" in social media

7. Make it easy for people to try you out

8. Run events, seminars, and teleseminars

9. Develop an effective follow-up system

10. Keep it personal

Branding Strategy #1:
Have a great Web site

When you position yourself as the expert in your market, you need to have a home where people can find you. While your business may well have a physical presence such as an office or store, these days, it's essential to have a powerful online presence. In short, if you don't have a Web site, you don't exist!

But here's the thing. Most businesses fail online because they don't have a clear idea of the purpose of their Web site. A Web site without a strategy is going nowhere. But when you get the strategy and the presence right, you have the keys to unlimited success.

A Web site is the perfect employee—working for you 24 hours a day, 365 days of the year, dealing with queries from prospects, taking orders, and delivering them.

So if you don't have the right kind of online presence, you are losing out on an infinite number of potential customers.

The right Web site features tools to attract prospective customers, make them want to find out more, and convinces them to give you that most valuable of commodities—their e-mail address—so that you can keep in touch and turn them into customers.

Here are my seven top tips for creating a great Web site and harness the full potential of a successful online presence.

#1: Capture their contact details

Here is the biggest mistake that most businesses make with their Web sites. They don't capture the details of their visitors. The harsh reality is that your Web site is one of billions out there, and most visitors will only pass once. So, if you miss the chance to get someone's details, you've probably lost any chance of making a connection.

On the other hand, if you capture the details of your visitors, you can keep in touch and market to them forever.

The customer is the real value of a business. However, until you get their name and contact information, you cannot establish a lasting relationship. So, if you aren't attempting to collect at least the e-mail address of every potential customer who comes to your Web site, you are wasting one of the greatest prospecting tools of our time. That's why you need a method of collecting the e-mail address of every person who lands on your Web site. The aim is to establish a way to keep in touch with them.

In order to get them to give you their e-mail address, you will almost certainly need to offer something in return, such as:

➢ Free newsletters

➢ Special reports or white papers

➢ Discounts

➢ Free trials

Once you have their contact information, you can build a relationship by staying in touch with them using automatic follow-up e-mails. The sign-up form should be prominent and simple—all you need to do is make clear what you are offering and invite people to sign up now.

#2: Make it easy to contact you

Something else that's crucial on your Web site is that you should make it easy for visitors to contact you. So on every page, you should have:

➢ Contact phone number (800 numbers are best)

➢ Contact e-mail address

The most effective way to show these is to put them at the top right of your Web page.

There are a couple of other ways to make it easy for people to contact you:

➢ Have a "contact us" form they can fill out and submit to you without needing to use e-mail

➢ Have an online chat facility if you have someone available who can deal with questions in that way.

#3: Add testimonials

There is no more powerful statement about your business than a third-party testimonial. If you walked into a business and saw hundreds of thank-you letters from clients all over the walls, you'd probably think you were in the right place.

It's the same on your Web site. If there are loads of testimonials from happy clients, you're going to take the business a lot more seriously.

Video testimonials are the most powerful of all but even audio and photos make a big difference. However, simple text testimonials are much better than having nothing at all.

Testimonials should always be genuine, and they should sound genuine. They are much more convincing when you have full details of the person providing the testimonial—include as much information as possible such as Name, Title, Company or Organization, City, State, Web address.

There is no such thing as too many testimonials!

#4: Provide news and information about your business

While you don't want to have your Web site dominated by boasting about your business, people want to know what you do and what you are up to. If you have a "Latest News" section on your Web site, it allows you to publish this kind of information in a way that seems natural. Here, you can include information such as recent large contracts won, charitable involvement, new people joining, and important company dates and events—e.g., millionth customer, 25th anniversary. You should report this information in the third person and without too much hype so that it comes across as news.

You should also make sure your site has enough basic information about your business to reassure people that you are to be taken seriously.

Make sure you include essential information about your business, such as when it was founded, where you are located, who the key management are, who some of your customers are—and, of course, what you do.

Try to bring the business to life with a few well chosen photos such as your office or store, your products, key people, events you have attended (such as trade shows, symposiums, or seminars), and social events featuring staff or clients.

This is your chance to make a great first impression. You want to treat people as if they were walking in your door for the first time. You should give them a real sense of who you are, what you do, and what makes you special. You want to make them feel comfortable about doing business with you, even though they are only visiting your Web site. Helping them feel as though they are doing business with real people goes a long way to building trust and confidence in the online world.

#5: Answer frequently asked questions

When people visit your Web site, they may come up with reasons why they won't do business with you. In face-to-face sales, these are known as "objections," and you can deal with them at the time.

Online, you don't have the opportunity to handle these objections directly but they will still arise. People will have their own questions but—because no one is there to answer them—they will make up their own answers.

However, the reality is that the same questions will come up on a regular basis, and you can provide the answers to these using a "Frequently Asked Questions" (FAQ) page.

Quite simply, this lists the most common questions or objections that clients have and provides the answers. Having their question answered in this way can overcome the fears and concerns a prospect might have about doing business with you.

#6: Let them buy your products and services

A huge percentage of purchases are now being made online as people become more comfortable with the process. Therefore, if possible, you should give people the opportunity to buy direct from your Web site. It's not possible with every business, but often it is possible to create special products or adapt existing ones so that you can deliver them online. It's a great way to make sales around the clock and give a much wider range of people the chance to do business with you.

#7: Plan your Web site design and layout carefully

One of the keys to having an appealing Web site is that it should be attractive and easy to use. That doesn't mean you have to spend a fortune on fancy design and gimmicks. However, you do need to take time and plan it to make sure it suits your needs.

Start by gathering examples of other sites you like. Notice how they are laid out and identify what sites do well and do badly. Then you can start creating a content outline. Make a note of the key pages you will need such as:

➢ Testimonials

➢ About us

➢ Contact

➢ FAQ

➢ Products

As you build up your list of main pag~
included on each page. For example, your
include:

➢ Description of what you do

➢ Pictures of your key people

➢ Your best testimonials

➢ List of key products

A Web designer should have a good eye for visual appearance and
will be able to advise you on the best way to build your site to
meet your goals.

Remember, it's your business, and you know what you want.
You should be willing to ask for advice but don't be talked into
unnecessary, expensive steps just because they look good or are
the latest fad.

Your Web site should be an extension of how your company
appears in the off-line world. It should therefore reflect your
brand—including the colors, logos, and typefaces you use off-
line.

year, our band had written our first original song and wanted to perform it in front of the biggest crowd possible. Then the lightbulb went off again ... it was close to the 4th of July, and there were two HUGE festivals being held locally that EVERYONE attended.

So I got the crazy idea to make a call to one of the organizers. I told him that I was the manager of a local band (that was true—Eric and I were comanagers).

Then I told him they were getting ready to relocate to Atlanta to "launch their first single" (kinda true. We WERE moving to Atlanta to go to music school, and we WOULD be "launching" our single ... somewhere. LOL).

Next, I told him the band wanted to debut their new single LIVE in front of their hometown before the rest of the world heard it! PLUS, if we could be grand marshals of the parade that morning, we would CONSIDER filming a live video for the song that day!

He was excited and agreed. We were grand marshals in the parade, performed our song live in front of an estimated 10,000 people, PLUS our girlfriends DID film a video for the song!

While I'm not proud of the half truths that I told to put us in the spotlight, I think the end result was worth it.

I learned another valuable lesson that day. A little creativity can take your local celebrity status a LONG way!

Branding Strategy #2:
Create a crowd-pulling blog

Blogs have now become an extremely popular way of quickly and easily publishing your views and ideas on a wide range of relevant topics. One of the great benefits of having a blog is that it allows you to communicate directly with your customers and prospects as they can comment on your posts and you can respond.

You can have a blog that stands separate from your Web site, or it can be linked to your site. A powerful advantage of having a blog as part of your Web site is that search engines love them. The search engine "spiders" from Google, Yahoo, Bing, and other search engines are software programs that "crawl" the Internet looking for new content.

They rank the content based on factors such as relevance to the search topic using a complex mathematical formula. Search engines love content that is updated regularly, so when you write often on a topic, your chances of being ranked highly will increase.

The content is ranked according to the "keywords" in your content. So when you write about keywords that are popular, your chances of coming up high in the search topics are increased.

Therefore, the more often you blog, the greater likelihood you will appear higher on a page when someone conducts a search using keywords related to your product or service.

But the real benefit of having a blog is the way it allows you to connect with real people—not just with search engines.

Here are three keys to getting the best from having a blog on your site:

➢ Post often

➢ Post about relevant topics

➢ Post using appropriate keywords

Below are some ways to make sure your blog is the best it can be.

➢ **Know your target audience:** Don't try to please everyone and don't write about material that isn't relevant to your target audience. If your topic is investment programs, don't write about music for teenagers. That might seem obvious but it's easy to stray off course. Choose the right language as well—if you are writing for CEOs, write in a professional style.

➢ **Keep it brief:** When people read online, their attention span is typically limited to about 100–300 words. They want useful tips and actionable answers. Over time, these short posts build credibility and interest.

➢ **Use lists and tips:** People love posts that give quick, easy information such as "How-To" guides or "Top 10" lists. It helps them identify steps they can take to apply the information in their own lives.

➢ **Position yourself as the expert:** Don't be afraid to share a few of your secrets to success. People love to hear about your success, but more important, they want to know how they can have it too. They will happily pay someone else to tell them what they need to do to get fast results. So make sure you tell people what they need to do to follow up with you.

> **Allow comments:** Encourage people to leave comments on your posts. Challenge readers to share their own experiences and opinions on what you have written. This is not only establishing communication between you and your readers; it is also building extra content that makes your site more interesting to others.

By the way, some people tell me they can't blog about their business because their boss/professional board/state law won't allow it. Fact is, in this situation, you just need to think out of the box. If there are certain things you can't talk about—talk about something else. There is bound to be something you can share that helps you build a distinctive expert brand.

Deciding what to write about

If you are looking for ideas on what to write about, it's a good idea to keep up-to-date with what is happening in your market. There's a simple, free, and widely available tool that can help you do that. It's called Google Alerts, and you can find it at: **www. google.com/alerts**.

It allows you to stay up-to-date with information on any topic that you want to keep track of. You can type any word into Google Alerts, and then, when Google indexes a new Web page that contains this, it alerts you.

Some great uses for Google Alerts are:

> Keeping track of trends and key issues in your industry

> ➢ Keeping tabs on who is talking about you and your business on blogs and Web sites

> ➢ Tracking where your press releases or articles are posted

> ➢ Monitoring your competitors

Blog promotion

One of the best ways to promote your business and build your expert status is to syndicate your blog. There are many tools for doing this, but one of the easiest to use is **www.feedburner.com**.

Feedburner and similar tools turn your blog content into what is known as an RSS feed—this stands for Really Simple Syndication. Users can subscribe to your feed and view your content in their own RSS reader without having to go directly to your site to read your content.

Google Reader is one of the most popular RSS readers and makes it easy to keep track of content from a number of sources.

If you're not already using an RSS reader to view content, subscribe to Google Reader or something similar and you'll see why it is so valuable.

If you use iGoogle, you can have the content published direct to your personalized page.

To get people to subscribe to the content from your blog, you'll need to build up their trust over time and demonstrate that you are delivering valuable content. However, when you build your build your local celebrity status and define your expert brand, you'll start attracting a growing number of subscribers to your blog.

My Personal Branding Story Part 5

*While this isn't exactly a personal **branding** story, it is very **personal** and will help explain how I began my journey back into my families automotive business—even though my parents practically begged me not to. They told me I could stay home and work for the family car dealership, but I refused. So I had to look for a part-time job for some extra money.*

I tried the mall and waiting tables but found nothing where I could make the money I wanted. Then I saw an ad in the paper for a Toyota/Buick dealership that was looking for salespeople and you could make up to $75k a year! I didn't really want to sell cars but knew I could—and I liked the sound of the money—so I applied. I got the job!

I went to school from 8 a.m. until 1 p.m., and then sold cars from 3 p.m. until midnight. In the first month, I made $4,800 selling cars and was also a full-time student! I was hooked.

The second month, I made $6,000! I quit school and worked there an entire year before telling my dad what I was doing for income and how much I loved it. I was scared that he would kill me, but I told him I wanted to come home and sell cars for the family dealership.

So I showed up for my first day of work at Frank Myers Auto in my smart clothes, and my dad told me I was a little overdressed for the detail dept. WHAT?!

He said he wasn't starting me at the top just because I was his son. So I went from making $60k a year in my early 20s to making $8 an hour.

I did that for a year and waited for a sales position to come open. One day while washing a car, I looked on the lot and saw a father and son getting ready to leave. I thought to myself ... "I've got to get out of this detail shop and here's my chance."

So I ran out to them in my galoshes and had my rubber gloves on and sold them a car. My dad accepted that I was finally ready and moved me into sales.

The rest, as they say, is history.

Personal Branding Strategy #3: Generate loads of publicity

One of the most effective ways of building your expert brand is through the power of publicity. With the right approach, you can achieve a great deal, even with a fairly limited budget. Clearly, it's the favored technique of the music and movie stars. They want to hit the front pages and make sure they're being talked about.

It's the same in your business, but you do need to make sure you have a message that is both newsworthy and helps establish your expertise.

Issuing press releases

The main tool for generating publicity is issuing a press release to your target media. You can do this when you have something newsworthy to announce.

Editors are not interested in you or your story—they want to know what's in it for their readers. So you're not going to get much coverage for publishing your latest monthly newsletter, but you may when you have an angle such as:

> ➤ A major event

> ➤ A significant new product or service
> ➤ A controversial opinion on a current topic

One great way to attract publicity is to create some sort of event that attracts media interest. Any business can do something like this. The key is to find a theme and run with it. You can easily tie it in with current news events or with normal holidays in the calendar.

The media are always interested when someone they see as an expert has a strong view on something happening in the news, such as changes in the law.

Another great way to get free publicity is to link up with a charity or nonprofit organization.

It's a lot easier to pitch a press release or idea if you already know someone on the inside, so it can be worth investing time in getting to know your local reporters and editors or those who write about your topic in trade and national media.

Submitting press releases to news outlets, such as newspapers, magazines, periodicals, trade journals, television stations, and radio stations, gives you a good chance of media coverage.

When you get media coverage, this effectively acts as independent endorsement of your expertise and makes a big contribution to building your local celebrity status.

If you want more chance of coverage, you may decide to hire a public relations firm to handle this for you—even for a one-off event. Another option is to hire a professional writer to create your press release using a Web site such as **www.elance.com**.

Online publicity

The main reason for sending out press releases is that you want to attract the attention of the media and have them write up the details of your announcement—perhaps even interview you. However, an added benefit is that syndicating press releases online can generate valuable links back to your Web site.

There are several Web sites that make it easy for you to syndicate your press releases online, such as:

www.prlog.org — free but very effective

www.prweb.com — offers several levels of service, including podcasting and search engine optimization

www.prnewswire.com — also offers more advanced services depending on your needs

Once you write a press release, you should also post it in a "latest news" section of your Web site.

My Personal Branding Story—Part 6

The government's Cash for Clunkers campaign was the most successful promotion in the history of the automotive industry. As soon as it was announced, I realized how big it was going to be. The only problem was the money was only going to new car dealers not used car dealers.

So I instantly began plotting how my dealership could take advantage of Cash for Clunkers without the government's assistance. I teamed up with a couple of my marketing mentors, Jimmy Vee and Travis Miller*, *and we decided to play the classic David v. Goliath story (or the small-business owner v. big government).*

I sent out a press release to all of the local media outlets outlining my disgust with Cash for Clunkers. I said the program discriminated against hardworking Americans that didn't want or couldn't afford a new car ... not to mention it discriminated against used car dealers.

I also announced that I was putting up $100,000 of my own money to fund a program to help out the people that didn't qualify for Cash for Clunkers!

I rolled out our Cash for JUNKERS campaign within days of the original Cash for Clunkers program, and the response was more than I ever expected.

On the second day, I counted more than 70 people at the dealership at once! And that wasn't counting the employees.

At the end of the fifth day, I announced the $100,000 was already gone and I was putting up another $150,000! That's when the unexpected happened and I got a call from the Fox News Network. A producer had been forwarded the original press release and asked me if I would be a guest on their morning news program to talk about Cash for Junkers.

Of course, I agreed, and 4 days later, Fox News did a 3-minute interview with me that was broadcast live across the United States. One of the local news affiliates picked up the story the same afternoon. I then parlayed that appearance on a national news program into a spot with the local and national media as a top "go-to guy" in the automotive industry.

After the Fox News interview, I appeared on NBC, CBS, and ABC affiliates across the country as an industry expert.

I've written for the Fast Company and Edmunds blogs, as well as been featured in the WSJ.

I'm not telling you all of this to brag. I want you to know how easy it is to build your local celebrity status and leverage the influence you have to crush your competition.

This story started out by repurposing someone else's great idea and making it my own. Once we had the idea, we simply wrote a press release to let everyone know about it. I don't think it gets any easier than that.

*Author's Note: Jimmy Vee & Travis Miller are not only my friends and marketing mentors, they are also the nation's leading experts on attracting customers, the founders of Gravitational Marketing and the co-author's of the excellent book "Gravitational Marketing". I highly recommend you go buy their book NOW!

Personal Branding Strategy #4:
Publish a newsletter people want to read

Keeping in regular touch with your network of customers and prospects is vital if you want to build deeper relationships. In fact, with the pace of information and change these days, it's essential to stay in front of them if you don't want them to forget about you! One of the best ways of maintaining that relationship is having your own newsletter. These days, many people do that through an online newsletter or "e-zine," and I'd strongly recommend that you have that as part of your strategy.

But, if you really want to make an impression, you should consider a printed newsletter delivered through the mail. Many people reject this idea because they worry about the printing and distribution costs. But the fact is—people love to get things in the mail, and they don't have time to read all their e-mails.

So, if you want to get noticed and remembered, a printed newsletter is a powerful tool. Yes, I'm talking something printed on real paper that you can mail to your clients and prospects and hand out to everyone you meet.

Depending on your business and your needs, you may opt for a glossy color edition with lots of photos, or it may be simply something printed in black and white on your laser printer. The key is to provide valuable information so that you stay front of people's minds.

You can give people information about what's going on in your marketplace and share tips on how to get better results. The possibilities are endless, and this works in every industry! It works for dentists, attorneys, retailers, carpet cleaners, massage therapists, restaurants, and just about every type of business.

Your newsletter can be as long or as short as you'd like. You can include:

➢ Success stories from past clients

➢ Congratulations to clients who have used your product or service successfully to change their life

➢ Coupons for discounts on a featured product or service

A newsletter is essentially a way for you to speak to all of your clients and prospects every month to let them know how you can help them, just like you've been helping others. Remember, people like to receive something they value—not junk mail—so you must make sure that you are delivering worthwhile content that people can use.

You may even choose to do online and off-line versions of your newsletter as people's preferences vary. Some like everything online, while others prefer to hold things in their hands.

Something that may surprise you is how much your clients will love their newsletter. Try missing a month or dropping a popular feature and you'll soon get many calls.

What would you give to have loyal fans like that?

My Personal Branding Story Part 7

Our company newspaper The World Enquirer *was intentionally modeled after the* National Enquirer *gossip tabloid with big, bold, attention-grabbing headlines. I wanted to stand out in a crowded automotive marketplace. I felt the best way to do that was to produce something that didn't look anything like a car dealer ad.*

I sent out 15,000 copies of the first issue. They were four full-color pages on newspaper stock and cost .28 cents each in the mailbox for a total of $4,200! I filled the newspaper with 800 phone numbers, silly pictures of the staff dressed up in ridiculous costumes, and HUGE offers. We dropped them over the course of 4 weeks so we could create some "extra" opportunities.

Little did I know that it would yield a whopping 5 percent response ... an average direct mail piece generates 1–3 percent. That's an EXTRA 175 opportunities a week that resulted in the following averages: 88 appointments, 44 shows, and 22 vehicles sold! The ROI was 20X.

Needless to say, I produced another World Enquirer *every 4 weeks until it burnt itself out 2 years later.*

Personal Branding Strategy #5:
Write an expert book

If you want to establish credibility fast in your field, there are few better ways than writing a book. When you write a book, you effectively have your prospective client's attention for several hours—giving you the chance to share your business philosophy and outline how you can help them. When you have great content, you will immediately stand out from the competition—just by having published a book. Giving out your book to potential customers is just like handing over a 200-page business card. It will really impress them.

Most people never question the authority of a book. If someone writes a book, they are automatically viewed as an authority.

Of course, writing a book may seem like a daunting task. That's why most people don't do it. However, when you break it down into smaller chunks it is much easier. Here are some examples:

- Write a series of articles on your chosen topic that, over time, will build into a book

- Create a series of special reports on various topics that later form the chapters for your book

- Use content you create for blog posts, newsletter articles, and articles for external publication

Since you will be creating this type of content anyway, this approach gives you a reason to create the content that will later become your book.

You can certainly write all of your own content for your book, but if you don't like writing or simply don't have the time, you can hire someone to write it for you. You can find these people—called ghostwriters—locally or by searching for them online. One easy way to find several is by using sites such as **www.elance.com**.

Another great strategy for creating content is to follow the formula that created multimillion-dollar success for Jack Canfield and Mark Victor Hansen with their *Chicken Soup* series. They got people from all around the world to submit their own stories. Then they compiled these stories into books, printed them, and sold them.

You can do the same thing!

➢ How about having each of your clients write a case study about working with you?

➢ Or you could contact experts in each field that you want to cover and invite them to submit a chapter to be published in your book.

By having multiple people take on the burden of writing chapters of the book, you greatly lessen the burden on yourself.

Once you have created the content, most people think it is difficult and expensive to publish a book or that you have to get a publishing deal. However, it is now much easier than ever before. You can self-publish your book by having it printed by a printing company that specializes in books. You can find many such companies online. One popular option is **www.CreateSpace.com**, which is owned by Amazon.com and offers all of the services you need to publish your book. They will even sell it on Amazon.com for you!

My Personal Branding Story Part 8

I co-authored my first book with Jimmy Vee and Travis Miller and it was named Car Buying Secrets Exposed—The Dirty Little Tricks of a Used Car Dealer. *I created a 30-minute workshop/seminar based on the content in the book and gave it to hundreds (if not thousands) of civic organizations, churches, schools, etc. At the end of every seminar, I would give everyone a free copy of my book.*

*The question I get asked the most is "How much did I get paid for the seminars?" The answer is nothing. The books even cost me a few bucks each, so I actually LOST money each time I spoke. However, I was building my celebrity status and establishing myself as **the** "go-to" expert in my marketplace.*

At one point, the book fell into the hands of an editor from the big daily paper in town and I became her "go-to" guy for any story related to the auto industry.

On weekends, I would even go into the local "big box" bookstore chains and put my book on the shelves. While I'm not sure that they ever sold them, they were never there when I went back!

I eventually condensed the book into a "teaser" free report that my sales pros give away in the dealerships. They only cost about 22 cents (a little more than a business card) to make but bring back endless results.

Branding Strategy #6:
Make a splash in social media

These days, one of the best ways of building a powerful expert brand is through social media. It allows you to reach large volumes of people quickly—though you can also target very specifically to reach out to your ideal customers.

Another great advantage of social media is that it can provide a link between your business life and you as a person that is a valuable way to let people find out who you really are.

One of the big challenges of social media is discovering how to use it effectively without having it take over your life.

The three most popular social media tools are currently Facebook, LinkedIn and Twitter.

Facebook

With more than 500 million daily active users, Facebook is fast becoming the world's most popular place to hang out. Users typically log in to Facebook several times a day, and it has become a more important method of communication than e-mail for many.

Facebook makes the distinction between personal profiles and business fan pages. Personal profiles are all about you, and are where you should connect with your family, friends, and anyone else you want to. Fan pages are for brands, products, artists, a web site or an organization.

Some people prefer to keep their Facebook for family and real friends only, while others are happy to open it up to business contacts and customers. The advantage of opening it up is that customers and prospects get to know more about you, and you get the chance to connect with a wider range of people.

You cannot use a personal profile to promote your business so you should set up a separate Facebook fan page for your business. You can use your page as an information portal where people can find out more about your business and what you are up to. You can also set up a page as a public figure to help grow your expert brand, you may want to set up a page devoted to that. You can publish articles, videos, and virtually anything that people might want to know about your business.

You want to invite people to "Like" your page, and you should find reasons to attract them back regularly—such as gifts and competitions.

LinkedIn

LinkedIn has become very important for business-to-business connections. It has a very wide range of options that give you a great opportunity to build your brand.

The first step is making sure your profile is as complete as possible. The next step is then to connect with people. Start by linking up with people you already know, then join and participate in relevant groups.

Make sure you take time to engage with people and add value— remember, your objective is to build your expert status, so set out to help people. One way to do this is by answering questions in groups. In due course, you may even decide to establish your own groups.

Twitter

While Twitter is very popular, it's important to note there are many industries where it is very powerful and others where it is probably not so useful. However, it's a matter of creativity and effective use.

There is no point in setting up a Twitter account and then not tweeting. The whole point of having a Twitter account is to build up a group of followers. And if you are not tweeting regularly, then no one is going to follow you.

A tweet is simply a post of less than 140 characters and can be a short, interesting message—such as a quote—or a link to an online resource that you have found useful. Over time, your aim is to establish yourself as a respected source of information.

In order to build a list of followers, you need to start by following others. But remember that quality is more important than quantity. It's far better to have 100 of your ideal customers following you than thousands of people who will never be interested in you or your business.

Many people miss out on one of the main benefits of Twitter, which is that you can make contact with people directly, rather than simply sending out lots of tweets. You can send them a personal message or retweet one of their messages so that you get noticed.

It's often possible to make contact with people on Twitter that you'd never reach in any other way.

Getting a Return on Your Investment

The big question I always get asked about social media is what's the Return on Investment?

My answer is you'll have the same ROI with social media as with word of mouth. The only difference is that the influence of social media travels further distances at a greater rate of speed and has a tendency to have more impact.

With that being said, the best way to measure the ROI of your social media initiatives is to move away from an "old-school" balance sheet profit mentality and shift to a "new-school" social media public relationship mentality.

In other words, don't measure its success based solely on dollars and cents. Instead, measure success based on the number of comments, mentions, links, and stories that eventually emerge from your social media efforts.

My Top Social Media Tips To Define Your Expert Brand And Build Your Celebrity Status

Here are a few practical tips on defining your expert brand and building your local celebrity status with social media.

- **Never, Never, Never Spam (EVER!)**
  Several of my best friends on Facebook are car dealers. A couple of them are brilliant at engaging with their social media initiatives. The others are horrible. They don't create a dialogue, and they never engage with anyone. Instead, they insist on spamming my Facebook wall with their inventory. Remember, there is nothing social or

engaging about classified ads.

- **Use A Picture For Your Avatar, Not A Logo**
  Why? People buy from people ... not logos.

  While there are several "big box" companies that successfully use a logo for their avatar (such as Starbucks and Dell), using a professional photograph shows that you're a real person and allows people to connect with you on a personal level.

  Note: If you are a representative of a previously mentioned "big box" company, you may have to use their logo instead of your picture. That's OK. That makes it even more important to create a personal page and become the "unofficial" spokesperson/advocate for your brand. Remember, there is more than one way to skin a cat.

- **Update Your Page/Status Frequently**
  When you set up your fan page or Twitter account, don't leave it to stagnate for months on end. Your clients or customers do not want to associate themselves with people, brands, or businesses that don't engage.

- **Be Creative, Have Fun & Offer Incentives On Your Page**
  Get your friends, followers, or fans excited about you, your company, your service, or your brand by having contests, offering coupons, and giving free samples.

- **Engage In The Conversation**
  Remember to create a dialogue and not a monologue. It's called "social" media for a reason.

BONUS TIP: The Secret Formula I Used On Facebook To Generate $500,000 In EXTRA Income For My Business

Before I give you my bonus tip, allow me to address one thing. Yes, I realize I told you not to measure social media success based solely on dollars and cents.

However, if you can grasp the "new-school" social media relationship mentality I also spoke of, you can generate a huge ROI over time. Last year, my business generated $500,000 in additional income using the secret Facebook formula that I am getting ready to share with you.

Here is what I did ... step-by-step.

I. I created a Personal Facebook Page two years before I created a fan page

Why? To meet new friends, to reconnect with old ones, to establish my "voice" as the go-to expert in my field, and to introduce myself as the brand of my business.

2. I followed "The Rule of Thirds" when posting

- **One-third of my posts were about my business:** I recognized right away that people loved seeing behind the scenes of my business.

  I posted pictures of new team members in training class and several people posted comments wishing them good luck.

When I posted a picture of my management team getting the store ready after-hours for a big sales event the next day, it got many comments.

I also posted "How-To" videos, such as how to buy a car and not get ripped off.

These were easy to do and very effective. The information came from my book, which I later broke into sections for my blog, and then I filmed 2–5 minute segments with a handheld Flip camera.

Then I simply uploaded them to YouTube for hosting and posted the link on Facebook. Voilà! Instant engagement AND celebrity, all in one.

- **One-third of my posts were about personal things like my family:** I posted about movies that I had seen over the weekend and got into some very spirited debates.

One weekend I mentioned that I was going to see *The Last Airbender* with my 8-year-old son. When I came out of the theatre, I had more than a hundred comments and private messages.

It seems that people either passionately loved this movie or hated it. It didn't matter to me. These people were engaged in a conversation on my wall, and I loved it.

- **One-third of my posts were like an episode of the TV show *Seinfeld* and were about nothing.**

I posted weird holidays, my favorite recipes, funny videos

from YouTube ... I posted anything that was interesting or entertaining.

By the way, you can also follow "The Rule of Thirds" with your newsletters as well. It works like a charm.

3. I entered into as many conversations being held by other people as possible

I commented on other people's photos ("Beautiful pic. Thanks for sharing.")

I asked questions ("What did you think of that movie?"), and I "Liked" all types of posts.

My rule of thumb is 5-to-1, which means for every post, you comment on at least 5 others.

4. I attempted to make 10 new friends a day and sought them out by association

I discovered the easiest way to find Facebook friends was to seek out my real-life friends first. Then I sought out Facebook friends in the following order:

➢ Business associates, including my employees

➢ People I knew from church. This works especially well if you attend a bigger church

➢ People I knew from professional associations, such as Jaycees, Kiwanis, Rotary, Chamber of Commerce, etc.

➤ Former classmates

➤ I searched my e-mail address using Facebook's friend finder

After all of this, I had only about 150 friends. Now what? I searched my Facebook friends' lists and invited their friends to be my friends. Most of them accepted my request simply because we had at least one mutual friend.

Once they accepted my request, I attempted to enter into a conversation with them and show them that they were more than a number to me. Some liked it and returned the favor. Some ignored me like the plague. Kind of like real relationships, huh?

5. I continued this formula until I reached 2,500 friends.

It took me two years, and then I built a fan page. The two years in between, I started two blogs and invited my Facebook friends to read them. They did. These initiatives together made my company an additional $500,000 last year. I call it "additional" money because it wasn't there before Facebook. Actually, it was somewhere, but Facebook helped me find it, and you can find it as well.

It also helped increase the worth of me as the brand by making me a social media celebrity. I've traveled the country and spoken to thousands of people about the successes I've experienced with social media. But I've never shared my "secret step-by-step" formula with anyone until now.

What happens with social media is that people start to see another dimension of who you really are. You give them bite-sized glimpses of your personality. The more you tell people, the more they'll get to know about you. This will increase the chances that they'll find something that interests them too. That makes it easier to connect with you.

The ultimate goal in building your expert brand is to help people find common ground with you. You've got to give people reasons to want to like you, reasons they'll be attracted to you, think they're like you, and ultimately trust you and do business with you.

My Personal Branding Story Part 9

I'm a huge fan of the 1938 Orson Welles War of the Worlds *radio broadcast. Welles played dance music and interrupted it a number of times by fake news bulletins reporting that a "huge flaming object" had dropped on a farm near Grover's Mill, New Jersey. As the audience listened to this simulation of a news broadcast, created with voice acting and sound effects, a portion of them concluded they were hearing an actual news account of an invasion from Mars.*

Next, people packed the roads, hid in cellars, loaded guns, even wrapped their heads in wet towels as protection from Martian poison gas. They were attempting to defend themselves against aliens, oblivious to the fact that they were acting out the role of the panic-stricken public that actually belonged in a radio play.

One recent Halloween, my good friends Jimmy Vee and Travis Miller came up with a brilliant idea that reminded me of Welles's original War of the Worlds. *A "strange thing" would be found in the trunk of a trade-in and, to see it in person, people would have to come to the dealership.*

I decided to use social media to take the idea to the marketplace. I started with small, daily teasers on Facebook in mid-September. By mid-October, I was getting more than 30 messages a day through Facebook inquiring about the "Strange Thing" ... "What is it?" "Have I called the police?" etc. Any question you can think of, I was getting it.

By the time Halloween rolled around, more than 50 people a day were visiting the dealership just to see what we had found in the trunk. Everywhere we went, the staff and I were asked if the "Strange Thing" was real or not.

Of course, we played the whole thing tongue-in-cheek and always responded by saying, "We don't know, but isn't it the strangest thing you've ever seen?"

The "Strange Thing" became so popular on Facebook, Twitter, and YouTube that a national publication did a story about it. This was a great example of how to take an 80-plus-year-old-idea like War of The Worlds *and repurpose it into a successful social media campaign. And I also used it to leverage my local celebrity status.*

Branding Strategy #7:
Make it easy for people to try you out

Building an expert brand does not happen overnight— it needs an ongoing process that helps you build deeper relationships with your customers and prospects. The exact way this happens will vary in different circumstances— some people will jump to being long-term clients virtually right away, while others will get to know you gradually—deepening the relationship step-by-step.

The reality is that few people will jump straight into deep relationships, so you need to establish a process that allows prospects to become involved with you in different ways. You have to create various "comfort levels" where different people can opt to experience your services in a way they feel is appropriate.

Over time, you want to see people choosing deeper levels of relationship and higher value services. Sometimes it's said that this process is like embarking on a romantic relationship. Not many people ask someone to marry them on the first date. Similarly, business relationships take time to develop. Prospective customers want to know a bit more about you before they get too far into a business relationship. They "want to go on a date" with you by trying out low-risk, low-cost services.

The fact is most people today are fed up of being bombarded with marketing messages and are very wary about making big-purchase decisions. Therefore, you need to have a system that introduces you and your product or service to potential clients in easily managed steps. This will give them a chance to get to know you, find out what you can do for them, and try additional services when they like what they see. That means you need to keep moving them through the process and try to keep the relationship going.

Here are some of the steps that may be involved in helping your potential clients deepen their relationship with your company.

➢ Allow them to subscribe to free e-zines, newsletters, or special reports

➢ Let them purchase a low-cost e-book

➢ Offer them a higher-value audio or video course

➢ Let them take part in a teleseminar, webinar, or in-store

workshop about new ideas or upcoming products

➤ Offer them in-store training on how to use your products

➤ Offer them the opportunity to become a one-on-one client—for example, by Offering a personal shopper

➤ Let them become a member of a club with special benefits

➤ Send them an invitation to join a VIP program—for example, by offering them a concierge

At one end of the process, there is no risk for the prospect as the offer is free. At the other end, the cost may be several thousand dollars, but the client is getting great value.

You are happy to have clients at any step in the process as you are able to help people at any stage, and every client could easily go to the more profitable steps in the process. Not every client will go through all the steps—some immediately prefer the higher-value, more personalized service—others will stay at the lower-cost end indefinitely.

And, never forget, someone who only subscribes to your free newsletter may well mention you to a friend who eventually buys one of your high-end products.

If you don't offer a range of ways for people to get to know you and deepen the relationship, you will miss out on potential contacts.

My Personal Branding Story Part 10

While working at the dealership, I continued to sing/write/perform music with my best friend Eric. We had formed another band that had garnered a good-size following on the East Coast. We continued to use our local celebrity influence to open doors for us.

Every time we played, we sent out press releases. We had a "fan club" that sent out a newsletter every month to folks on the mailing list. We would play gigs and take the show posters that were made at the local print shop, autograph them, number them, and have them laminated. Then we would sell them at the shows as "Limited Edition" signed and numbered collectors' items.

We would kick out inflated beach balls at one point during the concerts ... We knew that the fans would love it, but we also knew that the fans that ended up with the beach balls would come over to the merchandise stand after the show was over to get them signed and personalized. The more we kicked out, the more people would come to the merchandise stands for personalized autographs.

When our first CD came out, we wanted to get it in stores, so I would go to music stores and create a bin for it.

We could have played more than we were booked for, but we turned down small gigs all the time because we only wanted to play "BIG" shows. Then when we realized that a lot of the big gigs had dried up, we started having our own big-event concerts. We would rent out a local high school gym, book a pro sound and light company with video screens, and hire a couple of big signed music acts to be on the bill.

Little did they know but THEY would be opening up for US! On the posters and in the press, we booked ourselves as the headliner and the much-bigger signed bands as the special guests or the opening acts.

This gave us a lot more credibility and looked great in our bio! This is an example of the Power of Association Marketing at its best.

Branding Strategy #8:
Run events, seminars, and teleseminars

Just think—if you had the chance to speak to more than 100 of your ideal clients at one time, would you get some new business? I'd suggest there is a pretty good chance you would.

And that's exactly what happens when you speak at a trade show, seminar, or conference, and these are happening all the time, especially in major cities.

Live events

Many of these events will offer a potential audience of just the kind of people you want to be in front of. You may even have the chance of audiences of more than 1,000. Just speaking at one good seminar or trade show a month could get you in front of many more people than you could dream of seeing through networking or individual meetings.

And the key thing is that the organizers of these events are often looking out for interesting speakers who can bring a fresh topic to their conventions. So make sure you look out for details of events coming up in your area—especially those held by trade associations of which you are a member. When you attend trade shows, seminars, and events, hand out business cards, hoping people will remember you.

When you speak at these events, you'll find a line of people waiting to talk with you.

If you don't have suitable events happening in your area, you'll find it is worth travelling to attend them. Alternatively, you can quite easily put on your own events. You don't need hundreds of people in the audience—you just need the "right" people.

When you are the speaker, you automatically have credibility. Rather than taking time to visit your top prospects in their offices and trying to convince them to do business with you, you can get the same group of people together in a setting that makes them see you as the expert.

When they see others in the audience, it gives you the added credibility that all these people are also considering doing business with you. Instantly, you become the sought-after expert!

Teleseminars and webinars

One way of gaining many of the advantages of seminars is to run teleseminars. While they don't allow you to speak to your prospects face-to-face, they have other advantages—for example, people don't have to travel so your geographic reach is unlimited.

You've probably been on many teleseminars, and they are much easier to organize than you'd think. It's essentially a conference call where you invite people to listen in.

You can use teleseminars to deliver solid content (with no obvious pitches), and you can include some pitch either to launch a product or service or to build up anticipation for something to be released in the future.

You can even arrange a series of them as a teleclass and charge big money to attend.

With teleseminars, you can close off all of the lines if you want to be the only one speaking, and you can open them up when you'd like to take questions.

One good resource for teleseminars is **www.freeconferencecall. com**.

Webinars are similar to teleseminars but have the extra advantage of allowing people to see a presentation or demonstration on their computer.

Make sure you record your teleseminars and webinars so that you can re-purpose the content. You can develop them into products which you can sell on your Web site or at events.

My Personal Branding Story Part II

The reality about book signings is that no one cares except you, your family, and MAYBE a few choice friends. I knew this when I scheduled my first book signing and wanted to do something about it ... something different than every other "dud" of a book signing that I had ever seen.

So I hired people to show up at mine. "Extras," to be exact. Three hundred of them (in reality, 250 of them were paid. The others were family and friends).

However, I didn't pay them cash ... I used the barter system and gave them all a membership into the VIP Club at my dealership. It included a free oil change, four free car washes, discounts on parts & services, PLUS they got to be in a Frank Myers Auto Maxx TV commercial! I

*also hired a cameraman to take pics, a videographer to make a video,
a musician friend of mine to provide background music with his guitar,
and a catering friend of mine made some food and served punch.*

*It looked like a million dollars and garnered me an immeasurable amount
of celebrity "buzz." It only cost me a few thousand dollars.*

Branding Strategy #9:
Create a "get-to-know you" continuity campaign

The key to turning prospects into clients is allowing time to
develop a relationship with them. Few people will take out their
credit cards the first time they meet you. They need to take time
to find out more about you and what you can do for them.

One of the best ways of letting them do this is to create a "client
continuity campaign." These are drip campaigns where you stay in
front of your prospective clients on a regular basis and let them
get to know you a little better each time.

Here is an example of how you could develop such a campaign:

- **Month 1—Introductory Letter**

  This introduces you and your services and invites
  prospects to contact you to find out more, for example,
  by downloading a gift or special report from your Web
  site. You could also invite them to attend a special event
  in your area.

- **Month 2—Special Report**

  Here you can mail out a printed copy of a special report

about a topic that matters to your prospects. Give them just enough information to make them want to contact you to learn more. Make sure you include a strong "call to action" so they know they can contact you for more information.

- **Month 3—Customized Postcard**

Postcards are a very effective way to attract attention and encourage people to contact you. You should use them to invite people to request a free report or CD or to promote a specific product, service, or offer.

The big advantage of postcards is that people don't have to open them to read the message, and you can use strong graphics and powerful headlines to make a big impact.

- **Month 4—Product/Service Brochure**

Once people know you a little better, send out a more detailed overview of your products and services. This can contain successful case studies of past clients, plus special offers or coupons encouraging them to try out your services.

- **Month 5—Personal Interest Article**

This is a story about you or your business that looks as though it were taken right out of a magazine. It explains who you are, what you do, and how you are different from others in your industry. To make the article interesting, try to avoid the boring corporate profile and tell your story in a unique way. Demonstrate how you are revolutionizing your industry and getting great results for your clients.

- **Month 6—Audio CD**

  This is another opportunity to connect with your prospects in a unique and useful way. You can record a teaching session or have someone interview you.

  People like receiving audios as they can multitask and listen to them in their car or at the gym, rather than taking the time to read a report.

  While it's important to deliver quality content, you can use the time to promote a particular product or service.

This type of program will take you through the first few months, but it's important to sustain it on a regular basis. Just make sure your message is consistent throughout the whole campaign and focus on one thing each time. Don't dilute the impact by trying to get them to do lots of different things.

There is really no limit to the range of information you can send out to clients and prospects that they will find useful and which will promote your services.

If you are creative and come up with some distinct ideas, you are more likely to be noticed.

My Personal Branding Story Part 12

After a few years at the dealership, it had become apparent to my dad that I had a knack for marketing. So he gave me a budget and put me in charge.

From my days in the band, I liked to make everything an event, and I wanted something that my town had never seen before so I created the $99 Used Car Sale.

We would preregister people at the dealership for a week in advance for an opportunity to buy a car for as low as $99. We would have 150 vehicles on the lot and would mix in 4–6 cars priced at $99.

The folks that registered would get an entrance badge, stand in line and—when the gates were opened—would run to the vehicle that they would like to try to buy.

A few lucky people would get a car for $99. The rest would get a great deal and still be happy.

We hired a DJ to supply the music, and I was the MC. We surrounded the premises with yellow CAUTION tape to draw attention to the dealership and hired security guards dressed in all black clothing to police the premises all night to create mystery. We wouldn't even let anyone use the bathroom until the gates were open—we made them use the Porta-potty.

While I thought there would be lots of people there, I could never have imagined that more than 1,000 people would show up that day! It was a beautiful controlled chaos.

We started having it as an annual event (and are still doing it more than 15 years later) and garnered local and national TV news coverage, PLUS a national trade magazine did a story about it.

The success helped my brother and I start "Make Money Marketing," where we charged a hefty fee to show other dealerships how to emulate the $99 Used Car Sale at their stores.

Branding Strategy #10:
Write articles

Writing articles is a great way to demonstrate your expertise. When your articles appear in a respected publication, you are seen as having independent endorsement and automatically gain expert status.

It doesn't matter whether the articles are published in your local free paper or a global publication as long as you have something useful to say and are reaching your target market.

Articles can be anything from a short report to a lengthy feature, and they can appear in magazines, newspapers, e-zines, newsletters, you name it.

Each time you have an article published it helps build your expert brand. You don't even need to be a great writer; it's more important to have something to say.

If your articles are well received, you may even find yourself being invited to contribute a regular column. This is a great way to establish you as an expert in your field. Then, when you have articles published, you can send reprints to your clients and prospects to boost your credibility.

Online articles

Publishing articles online is a great way of getting them seen by a very wide audience easily. You can do this by syndicating your articles—having them published on multiple other Web sites.

The main attraction is that, while these articles must contain useful content rather than being like advertisements, they include a section at the end called a resource box. This may contain information about the author and a link back to your Web site. One benefit of this is that many people will click on the link and visit your Web site. If you have set up a sign-up box on your site, you will be able to capture many of their e-mail addresses.

An additional advantage of publishing articles in this way is that many of the article sites are rated highly by the search engines. The fact that the articles include a link back to your site boosts your search engine rankings.

Here is an example of a resource box:

Tracy Myers is founder of The Celebrity Academy, which publishes a monthly e-zine covering topics that everyone looking to build their business needs to know. If you're ready to take your business to the next level, get more FREE info now at www.TracyMyers.com.

Many article Web sites allow you to post your articles for free. Some of the most popular are:

www.ezinearticles.com

www.goarticles.com

www.articlesbase.com

In addition, there are services that allow you to quickly submit your article to hundreds of article sites automatically. Here are some of top article syndication sites:

www.isnare.com

www.articlemarketer.com

www.submityourarticle.com

My Personal Branding Story Part 12

I started writing "Beat the Dealer" for a local magazine before the book came out, but it really took off when the book was released and it later turned into a blog.

Five years later, it has appeared in three different local magazines, and I get close to 200 e-mails a month in my in-box asking me car-buying questions & tips.

The articles are usually regurgitated content from my blogs and my books and take me less than 30 minutes a month to write. The response I get is huge, cements my place as an expert in the automotive field, and costs me nothing.

Remember: most local publications are always looking for local content. If you don't provide it, someone will. Why shouldn't it be YOU?!

CHAPTER 5

Branding Yourself As The Go-To Expert: Bonus Strategies and Tips

So far, I've shared 10 top strategies that will help you build your define your expert brand and build your local celebrity status. However, the list doesn't end there. So, while I can't cover everything here, I wanted to highlight a few more ideas you could consider.

PPC (Pay per Click Advertising)

Buying pay-per-click ads can be a great way to generate large volumes of traffic to your Web site quickly. These are the ads that usually appear at the top and down the right side of the search page. It works as a sort of auction system. You place a bid on the keywords that you want to have your advertising linked to. The most popular keywords command the highest prices, and the amount you bid determines where your ad will appear on the search pages.

Normally you want your ad to appear on the first page of search results, as most people never even get to the second page. You can normally set a daily budget for your advertising so that you are not paying unlimited amounts. You will want to test a range of different keywords and ads to see what works best.

While PPC is a great way to drive traffic, it can also be expensive. There are many horror stories of people running up large bills without generating revenue.

You need to remember that you pay for the click and the click does not earn you money. You only earn money when the click turns into a sale. It can be a very useful process but don't rush into it without the proper guidance. Start out with low limits and adjust them as you go. When you find campaigns that work, they are likely to follow a consistent pattern so you can continue to get great results.

Send cards and Thank-You letters

When was the last time you got a birthday card in the mail from someone who wasn't related to you? It doesn't matter how old you are; it's nice to know someone is thinking of you.

So, if you want to make a positive impact with your clients, why not send them a card every year on their birthday? They will love it, and it's something nobody else will be doing for them.

You could also send out a thank-you note after your first meeting with prospective customers or send thank-you cards every time someone sends you a referral.

You can set up birthday campaigns, thank-you campaigns, referral campaigns, or any other kind of campaign that you want. To keep it personal, the ideal is to handwrite and hand address all of them. But most of us don't have time for handwriting these notes. An alternative is to have it handwritten by someone else or to use software that prints out to look like handwriting.

Host your own radio show

It's easy to forget that radio is still one of the most popular forms of mass media—whether people are listening in their car or at the gym or at home, you have an attentive audience. So make the most of it.

While you can certainly buy advertising time, a great strategy for building your profile is to have your own radio show. You can buy blocks of airtime on local stations for less than you'd probably think. Just make sure that you are broadcasting to your target demographic.

A radio show is a bit like an audio newsletter as you get a chance to connect with your prospective clients for a specific period of time each week. And when people hear someone on the radio, they automatically think they're an expert, just as if they'd published a book. After all, why would they be on the radio if they weren't an expert?

You can even have listeners call in to discuss topics you want to raise. It's a great way to leverage your time by consulting with thousands of people at the same time.

You can also record your show and re-purpose it for other uses—such as for creating podcasts, audio clips on your Web site or CDs to send to clients and prospects.

Radio can sometimes be the forgotten medium, but it's a great way to build your reputation in your community or market.

Testimonials

We talked about testimonials in the Web site section, but they are just as important off-line. When you say you are great, it is perceived as boasting. When others say you are an expert, it has a much more powerful impact.

So, whatever business you are in, start building your bank of testimonials as soon as possible. Normally, all you need to do is ask. When someone is satisfied with your service, they are usually quite happy to provide a testimonial.

Often people hold back because they don't know what to say. You can make this easy for them by asking a few simple questions to find out what they think. The answers give you your testimonial.

Alternatively, you could write something for them based on what they say and ask if it is an accurate reflection of what they think.

Remember, it's always a good idea to get permission in writing from people if you are going to use their testimonial. You should make clear you will use the information publically. This will avoid problems later.

Something to remember whether you use testimonials online or off-line is that you should aim to include a wide range of different people, including men and women of different races and occupations. Use full names and cities of origin, if possible.

People always relate more easily to someone who is like them in some way, so the wider the range of people you show in your testimonials, the more chance there is they will see someone as being like them.

Have great photographs

Obviously, initial impressions are a big part of your expert brand. Not everyone will get the chance to meet you in person, so a key aspect of the impression you make comes from your photographs. Therefore, it's well worth finding a great professional photographer to take your photo.

A good photographer will make you look "real." That's their professional skill. So don't just rush down to that little camera booth and have some snapshots taken.

Equally, don't go for "glamour" shots. You don't want to look posed and unapproachable. You want to appear warm and friendly. If you look like you're greeting your best friend, you will come across well.

However, photos aren't the only option; why not try something a little different ...

My Personal Branding Story Part 13

The revelation came to me one afternoon as I stood next to a man dressed as Uncle Sam. That man was my father, Frank, namesake of my great-grandfather who opened the first Frank Myers store more than 80 years ago.

My father was dressed up to do a television spot for a tax-day promotion when a videographer laughingly suggested that instead of Uncle Sam, they should call him Uncle Frank. So I said, "Hey, that's pretty cool. Let's use it."

So we changed all the lines. Instead of Uncle Sam, we just replaced it with Uncle Frank, again and again. And just like that, a brand was born.

Now a cartoon version of Uncle Frank, along with the dealership's slogan "Everybody rides," is everywhere—in TV and print ads, on business cards, calendars, promotional materials—and his impact has been unmistakable. He has become a familiar icon that has helped push the company's profile up, resulting in increased sales. In fact, Uncle Frank was so popular that every employee now has his or her own cartoon.

That's an example of how you can turn your brand into a "superhero," using cartoons to enhance your status.

Use a wide range of media

Your image is affected by all of the ways people can experience you—whether it's your business cards, your Web site, or your marketing material.

It's a good idea to present yourself to potential clients in as many different media as possible. This is important because people like to receive information in different ways. Some like to listen, others pay more attention to what they see, and some need to hold something in their hands. To reach the maximum number of people, you need to present yourself in auditory, visual, and kinesthetic categories. So don't just hand out a business card; pass out a CD or DVD as well.

When you understand that people want to receive information in different ways, you can see the importance of having different methods of telling people about what you do.

Publishing a book will reach certain people, while putting on a seminar is better for others. You want to convey a consistent brand to different people in different ways. Using a wide range of media offers many different ways people can meet you and become involved with your services.

My Personal Branding Story Part 14

The dealership had always sponsored some events when they came to town because they reached our demos very well. One was a rap/hip-hop concert that usually attracted 15k+ people to the Coliseum. The second was WWE events.

Every year when they would come to town and ask me for a sponsorship, I just said yes. I spent my money and got my logo on a sign. But one day, another lightbulb went off and I told them I would sponsor the event under one condition ... that they let me use one of their "celebrities" to endorse the dealership.

At first they said no (especially the hip-hop concert promoter). But when they couldn't find another sponsor, they came back to me and said yes. So I got WWE World Champ (and now movie star) John Cena, the then WWE Divas Champ Maria, and the greatest pro wrestler of all time (and my childhood hero) Ric Flair to do commercials for me, saying my locally legendary tagline, "Everybody Rides."

I had my picture taken with them, had them plastered in every paper, and issued press releases talking about it.

The hip-hop promoter gave me LL Cool J, who ended up being one of the nicest and most professional celebrities I've ever met.

Many years later, people still ask me about John Cena, Maria, Ric Flair, and LL Cool J.

A celebrity endorsement is not only easy, it is powerful. It gives you instant credibility, and their "celebrity" rubs off on you. And if you play your cards right, it could be free!

Creating and Using Your Personal Story To Establish Yourself As An Industry Expert

One of the keys to building a successful expert brand is to avoid hiding behind a corporate label and to allow your personality to shine through. I realize that not everybody feels comfortable with this initially. But the fact is when you open up about yourself and let your potential customers see who you really are, they will be more drawn to you and the brand will become stronger.

That's what I've sought to do in this book. I've shared some stories that I hope will help you get to know me better. The stories also demonstrate my experience and give you some examples of how I could help you.

But, more important, I wanted to demonstrate how sharing your personal story can make clear to people how you can help them.

It's true that this openness may mean some people will decide they don't want to work with you as they don't see a close match for their needs. This can be hard to accept at first as no one likes rejection—

especially when there is a potential business deal involved. However, you'll find that this process helps you identify with the people you want to have as your clients and who will be the people for whom you will get the best results.

In the long run, this works better for everyone as you get more of the clients you want, and the people who choose deliberately to work with you get better outcomes. To get this result, you need to be ready to share a bit of your personal story, and sometimes, that means you need to work it out first.

Why You Do What You Do

The first part of your personal story is working out why you do what you do. We touched on this earlier when we started looking at how to develop your brand, but the purpose of this question here is to help shape your personal story.

The reason you do what you do can be a powerful motivating force that encourages people to work with you. If your story resonates with them, they will see you as someone who can make a difference to them. If you can identify a story behind what you do, this can make a big difference, not only regarding your own motivation but also to the way others work with you. The results for you and for your clients could be enormous.

How You Explain What You Do

How do you explain to people what you do? This is an important part of the process of establishing your Expert Brand and defining the way you want people to see you.

Initial impressions can be hard to change, and that's why it's important to learn how to describe what you do well. One of the ways to look at this is to examine the words you use when someone asks what you do.

Do you know how to describe your expertise in a way that makes someone want to pay attention and learn more? When most people are asked what they do, they simply reply with a label—I'm an attorney; I'm a consultant; I'm a dentist ...

In those few seconds, someone will immediately pigeonhole you and decide whether your services are of any interest to them. Unless they happen to be looking for someone with that label at that exact moment, it will make no impact on them, and they will either change the subject or move on to the next person.

If you want to hold someone's attention for more than a nanosecond, you need to give an answer that shows what's in it for them.

Imagine you step into an elevator and you have just a few seconds to get your message across. Could you explain what you do in a way that gains the other person's attention and makes them interested to learn more?

For example, I could say that I'm a marketing consultant. How much better do you think the results are when I respond with a statement like:

> *"I help professionals develop an expert brand that makes them first choice in their market and helps them attract more clients and make more money."*

Do you think this would have more chance of attracting their attention? You bet it would! They are much more likely to follow up with: "Tell me more!"

Of course, it's not really about getting stuck in elevators. It's about networking and social events. It's about being prepared to make the right impression in the first few seconds so that you can hold somebody's attention. You have to get them to stop and think. You have to make them think in terms of how they could benefit from what you have to offer. If they are thinking, "Maybe I need some of that ..." you at least have an audience.

This approach also has the benefit that it helps you know if the person is not interested in what you are offering. You either want to get a ticket to another conversation or quickly establish that they have no interest.

If you can sum up what you do in a way that grabs people's attention, you are much closer to having them do business with you.

Showing How You Can Help

There is a key to sharing your personal story in a way that gets people's attention.

Here's an example:

> "Hi, I'm Bob. I'm 5'9", weigh 140 pounds, am very fit, and get as many dates as I want. I used to hate my life, but now I love every moment of every day."

The key to the first part of the story is that you are telling people who you are now. The problem is that these words can sound like bragging and turn people off. So the key is that the next part uses these magic words: *"but it hasn't always been this way."*

When you start to share how things used to be, it grabs people's attention. They can identify with your story.

> *"I used to be 450 pounds and felt everyone was laughing at me. It was hard to get out of bed every morning. I was lonely. I didn't have the confidence to go on a date."*

Then you move to the third part of your personal story—the secret.

> *"Until I discovered _____"*

The secret, of course, is usually the product or service that you're promoting, which can help others overcome their issue or "pain."

You tell them whatever it is that is the secret to solve their problem, which is followed up with the magic words, *"And now I can show you how you can do the same thing."*

Here is the four-step formula for sharing your personal story:

1. Establish how successful you are—make the audience think—I want to be like that

2. Explain that *"it wasn't always this way"*—tell them how you used to be just like them

3. Say *"until I discovered"* so that they are now dying to know the secret

4. Show them how *"you can do it too."* They'll be willing to pay for your secret if it relieves a great pain in their personal or professional life.

Your personal story allows you to show your personality as well as the reason why your audience should listen to you and follow what you have to say. When you show your personality, let people see who you really are and tell your personal story. Your business will just get bigger and better.

Are You Ready For the Celebrity Academy?

We've talked about why and how you'll benefit from creating your own expert brand. I now want to share how you can do that easily and effectively. I'm going to tell you about The Celebrity Academy.

You know, it's funny—people are often puzzled when I tell them I've opened an academy to coach people on how to build your local celebrity status and define your expert brand.

The thing is most Americans are obsessed with celebrities like Paris Hilton, Britney Spears, Oprah, or Dr. Phil. But, having read this far, you'll guess I'm talking about something different.

I coach entrepreneurs, CEOs, professionals, business owners and many others how to:

> ➤ Charge more for the same services they are offering now.
> ➤ Get the red-carpet media recognition their business deserves!
> ➤ Gain instant credibility.
> ➤ Lock out their competitors in their field of expertise.

> ➤ The secret to achieving that is building your local celebrity status and defining your expert brand.

Interested?

When you attend The Celebrity Academy, you'll learn a series of strategies so that people who are looking for what you have to offer will find you everywhere they turn. When these strategies are executed correctly, your prospects hardly know anyone else exists but you.

It's all about finding out first what your potential clients are searching for and how they're searching for it. I'll cover the strategies for that in detail. Next, I'll show you specific ways to make sure your ideal prospects will find you. Then I'll show you how to make sure your ideal prospects can learn more about you, your philosophy, why you're right for them, and how they can reach you.

I can do this for you because I use the exact same strategies that big Hollywood PR agents use to seed the media—online and off-line—with the information that I want my prospects and clients to know. It's one of the oldest strategies around, but it's been heavily guarded for years by Hollywood gatekeepers who want to keep the media, and the money, to themselves.

Now it's available to you when you become a graduate of The Celebrity Academy.

The Celebrity Academy Gives You the Red-Carpet Media Recognition Your Business Deserves!

I can show you how to get television appearances that will build your business, elevate your brand, and blow your competition out of the water.

Getting on TV can launch your business. There's no other media that gives you the amount of nationwide exposure you'll receive from a single television appearance.

Here's an example of how one TV appearance can change your life forever. Back in the mid-1990s, Oprah Winfrey was sued by the Texas Cattlemen's Association for defamation. Since jury selection is critical in a big trial, she hired a firm called Courtroom Sciences and they helped her attorneys choose the right jurors, assisted in mock trials for witness questioning, and ultimately played a major role in winning the case.

Shortly after the win at trial, Oprah invited the head of Courtroom Sciences on her show and that one appearance launched his career.

That man is Dr. Phil.

But how do you get booked on shows like Oprah, Ellen or The Today Show when you can't even get a show producer to return your phone calls? Will the right questions be asked to spotlight your expertise and focus on your knowledge? And how much of your two or three minutes of fame will end up on the cutting room floor?

Big name shows will air once and, when you try to get a copy of the show to use in your marketing materials, you'll probably have to shell out a couple thousand dollars for a license — to use your own TV footage!

Who needs that?

Fortunately, you don't have to go through that mess. What's the behind-the-scenes secret to making your TV appearances do the heavy lifting for you? It's simply this:

Having the ability to utilize each and every appearance to your marketing advantage without having to use your high school senior's college fund to do it.

The key to successful marketing – marketing that strikes a chord with your target audience – is frequency. The more they see you and listen to you, the more they'll like you, trust you, and turn to you as their #1 go-to expert.

The Celebrity Academy is the opportunity you need to finally build your local celebrity status, define your expert brand and leave your competition in the dust.

Imagine being able to …

- Place a TV show starring YOU on your website or blog

- Make DVDs of your appearances that you can add to your media kits or give away as bonus material

- Increase your credibility by being able to add "as seen on" to your resume

- Syndicating your TV appearance on video sites like YouTube, Revver, and Vimeo

- Increase traffic to your site by having a TV show linking to you

A TV appearance is all that stands between you and lucrative speaking contracts where you're asked to appear and offer your expert advice for a hungry crowd. Have you always wanted a 6 or 7-figure book deal? Being on TV is the first step to landing a fat advance.

Ready to change your business game forever? Let The Celebrity Academy be your ticket out of unknownsville to Red-Carpet Recognition. Show producers will call you instead of the other way around.

Here's what you'll experience with The Celebrity Academy:

➢ Media and acting coaches — like those the stars use — will teach you how to be a great television guest who is repeatedly called back to be on TV. One of the most important things to learn when you're on TV is how to sell without selling. You'll be amazed at how many viewers ... and even other TV shows ... contact you after they've watched you on TV.

➢ Get a set of professionally produced headshots by an award winning photographer. The best part of this is that you have the sole rights to use these photos any way you'd like – you'll never have to worry about contacting the photographer for permission or pay huge fees for a couple of copies.

➢ Star in a television show that will air across the country and receive a final, production-quality copy of your appearance on the show so you can put together a lead generation DVD. You can post this appearance on your website and blog as well as in a newsletter to your clients – add a "share this" button to that newsletter and your appearance will go viral like a California wildfire during Santa Ana wind season.

➢ A publicist just like the Hollywood stars use will prepare a press release about being invited to appear on the show. This alone will drive traffic to your website – maybe even increasing the visitor amount so much that Google analytics can't keep up.

➢ Hang out at a red-carpet worthy party with other business experts just like you where you'll network with people who can offer even more exposure for your expertise. This is the same kind of afterglow party you see Grammy, Oscar and Emmy nominees and winners attend. This party is preserved on film with professionally shot photos you can use on your web site and in your marketing materials.

➢ Show the world you're the only expert to call — You'll get the Hollywood elite treatment by walking the red carpet and being photographed by Celebrity Academy paparazzi. You'll get tons of great images to add to your website, blog and newsletter showing you elbow to elbow with other elite business owners.

➢ As an added bonus, we'll show you how to be an Award-Winning author in one of our hard cover books. Our crack publishing team will show you how to get your book written and published while you're tending to other things.

Graduating from The Celebrity Academy with honors is the icing on your business cake that will automatically make you the only expert others will seek out.

Your newly learned expert status will give you instant credibility that will be a dream come true.

Don't deny yourself the opportunity of a lifetime even a moment longer. The Celebrity Academy will give you everything you'll need – at a fraction of the cost – to be a sought after guest on TV shows and for radio interviews.

Do you have what it takes to be a part of our next class of graduates? Contact us today for an application to enroll in The Celebrity

Academy but don't wait a second longer because after the first 20 people enroll, the class will be closed and you'll lose this business building opportunity.

Isn't it time you took the first step toward this once-in-a-lifetime business changing opportunity?

Be sure to visit www.The CelebrityAcademy.com today to receive more information on how to reserve your spot.

Hopefully, I'll meet you during the next semester and always welcome your feedback.

Tracy E. Myers, CMD
www.TracyMyers.com
Tracy@TracyMyers.com
Call Toll-Free: 888-487-3390

26 Marketing Essentials You MUST Implement To Successfully Position Yourself As An Expert In Your Industry
by Tracy E. Myers, CMD
& Bruce Roffey

In this bonus section, we'll share 26 powerful tips for successfully positioning yourself as an expert in your industry and using them to attract your ideal customers and build profitable long-term relationships with them.

Ask for Feedback

In order to successfully position yourself as an expert in your industry and build a successful business around it, you need to seek constant feedback from your customers and others with an interest in your business.

While you should also do this through normal feedback and special research, a great way of getting more detailed feedback is to gather together a group of friends, family, and business associates whose opinions and judgment you value.

Every quarter, gather about a dozen of these people together in a room and ask them to critique every aspect of your business. This will give you very valuable and specific feedback in exchange for the price of a nice lunch.

You need to go into this with an open mind and don't be too thin-skinned. Don't take their comments personally. You want the truth and their constructive feedback so that you can make the improvements needed to move your business forward.

You'll find that people who are less closely involved in the business than you will spot problems—and opportunities—that you might miss.

If you have a great set of advisors, you can even ask their permission to publish their names on your stationary and on your Web site as your advisory board. This can give your business extra credibility.

Another way of getting valuable feedback is making it easy for your customers to complain about your business. Of course, nobody likes complaints, but they are one of the best ways of helping you to improve what you are doing.

It's often worth taking the time to call people up or send them a card or a survey checking that everything was fine or asking, "How are we doing?"

If there are any problems with your product or service, it's better to find out about them now—rather than wait until you have hundreds of unhappy customers or even bigger problems.

Business Cards—Make Them Memorable and Give Them to Everyone

Ordinary business cards are dull and boring and are often stacked in a pile and never referred to again. They may even be thrown away immediately.

Yet, business cards can be a powerful marketing opportunity. You can easily turn your business card into a minibrochure that promotes your business.

> ➤ A great business card will have:

> ➤ A picture of you or your product

> ➤ A special offer

> ➤ A call to action

If you need to include a map or other more detailed information, you can use the back of the card.

A good business card will get kept and will be working for you when you are not there.

Don't just keep your cards in your pocket. Give them to everyone— and give supplies to others to hand out. Give several cards to business associates who might be able to promote your business. And include your card in all mail you send out—yes, even in bills!

Sometimes it's a good idea to have variations of your business card for different people, such as:

> ➤ Potential customers

> ➤ Professional contacts

> ➤ Vendors

> ➤ Referrals

If business cards work well for you, they can work just as well for virtually everybody in your business.

Many people such as counter staff and drivers have contact with customers and potential customers. They're important enough for this tiny investment, and they'll be proud to leave your card with customers and prospects. They'll hand your cards over to a wide range of people, and you'll get your name in many more places.

Consistency and Commitment

No matter how great your message is, the chances are that people aren't going to remember it if you only tell them once. So you've got to keep repeating it over and over again. That means you won't get maximum results by just sending one letter or e-mail.

If you are sending e-mails, you need to create a sequence so that you are constantly reminding people of who you are and how you can help them. You want to be there in front of them when they need what you are offering.

With direct mail and postcards, you need to be committed to sending them regularly to the same people. Your message needs to be consistent so that it sticks in the mind, but you need to find different ways of expressing it so that you reinforce it and maintain interest.

When advertising, it's rarely a good idea to just advertise once. You need a consistent presence. It's often best to advertise where you can afford to do it regularly—a small ad consistently appearing in the same place in a newspaper or magazine is likely to bring you better results than one big hit.

Deadlines

One of the most effective ways to get people to take action is by setting deadlines and limits. People are much more likely to do something if they know an offer is running out on a specific date or if the number of products or places available at a good price is limited. So make sure you put a closing date on any promotions—e.g., 20 percent off until 30 June. But choose your expiration date carefully—closing an offer on a Friday may cost you all the business you might have received over the weekend.

Easy to Contact

You want to make it as easy for people to contact you as possible. To do that, you need to make sure your company name, address, fax number, Web site, and e-mail details are on all materials, including simple items like packing slips and invoices.

Contact information should be very clear in any publicity and advertising. The whole point is that you want others to contact you.

If you are in touch with someone regularly, give them a business card so they can put it in their Rolodex or scan it into their computer. If they can't find your name, they may find your competitor's instead.

Fear

Of course, you don't really want to be going around scaring people. But often you have a responsibility to make people aware of the consequences of not taking action.

In many fields—such as security, personal safety, health, and investment—fear can be a good way of attracting attention and building your sales. But if you are going to use fear to get people's attention, make sure you have a solution that will help them remove that fear.

Often you need to make people recognize what they will miss out on if they don't buy your product or service. That could be as simple as fear that they will miss out on a bargain, but it may be fear of something more serious. Either way, fear of loss is usually more powerful as a marketing message than expectation of gain.

Give Customers What They Want

The best way to get plenty of customers is to give them exactly what they want. In order to do that, you need to have a very clear idea of who you are selling to and how you can meet their needs.

You need to start by defining very clearly the kind of person who is most likely to want or need your product or service. Then you need to establish some good reasons why should they want to buy it.

When you know who you are selling to—and why they would want what you offer—you can target your offer and your message to precisely the right customer base.

Both of these are important because even if you have a good product, if you fail to identify the correct motivation to buy, you won't maximize your potential. For example, one pharmaceutical company dropped an unsuccessful cold medicine because they couldn't solve the problem of the drowsiness it caused. Then somebody decide to market it as a bedtime cold medicine. They called it NyQuil, and it became the largest-selling cold medicine in its market.

So not only must you have a great product, but you also need to make sure it's positioned correctly.

A great way of finding out more about what your customers want is to pay attention to questions new customers ask you. If they ask you lots of questions about service, exchanges, and return policies, for example, they may be telling you about unpleasant experiences with a previous company. Arm your employees with details of key phrases and messages to look out for so that they can give a proper response. That will help you let these customers know you will solve the problem with no hassles.

Happy Birthday and Thank You

Personal contact with your customers makes all the difference. Mailing them greeting cards on special occasions like their birthdays shows that you relate to them as individuals rather than just one of a crowd. If you don't already have information about their birthday, send them a survey or offer that requests that information.

Inside the birthday card, you should include a coupon or special offer. Tell them it's a great opportunity to give themselves a gift.

Other holidays and special occasions also present opportunities for targeted mailings.

There is no better reason for sending someone a card or a gift than the chance to say "Thank You." Whether you are thanking them for their business or for a referral or for their help, people appreciate the fact that you took the time to do so. And it means they will be more likely to support you again.

People who refer business to you deserve a special thank you. You can do that in a range of ways, from a personalized thank-you card or phone call to flowers, dinner, a prize draw, or, in some circumstances, even a commission.

Don't forget that you shouldn't only thank your customers and people who bring you business. There are many others who contribute to your business success, so thank your reliable suppliers with a letter and give them increased orders.

Everybody appreciates a thank you. Even although it's worth doing for its own sake, it will help your business.

Impress with Testimonials

People are more likely to respond to your advertising message if they hear it supported by others rather than coming just from you. That's why one of the most powerful marketing techniques you can use is testimonials from previous customers.

A testimonial is simply a short message from people who have previously used your product or service, and they share how their lives are better for it.

Most people who are satisfied customers will be happy to give you a testimonial. However, people are busy and sometimes don't know what to say. So it can sometimes help if you offer to write something for them, and then get them to approve or adapt it.

Great testimonials address the concerns and questions that people have in their minds. When they see that someone else has got a good result, it helps break down resistance.

Join Up with Other Businesses

The costs of larger-scale marketing campaigns can sometimes be prohibitive for small businesses. But there is a great way to cut your costs, and that is to share them with others.

Chances are there are other businesses that want to reach the same people as you, and who are not direct competitors. When you share costs with others, it can reduce the costs considerably for everybody. That means high-quality printing, larger ads, and mailings to larger groups become more accessible and affordable.

You can even take this approach further than sharing marketing costs and think about how your products and services could be combined to offer a better solution.

Kids

There may be times when you have a one-off project where you need some temporary help. Maybe you want to deliver an in-house mailing or need help moving the business. Instead of hiring part-time workers from a temp agency, check with the local high school or university. Chances are you'll be able to find responsible young people who can help you out, perhaps in exchange for a donation to a school project. The cost to you may even be tax deductible but check with your accountant.

Sponsoring local kids' sports teams is also a great way to promote your business and support the local community. The parents of the kids on the team may well be potential—or existing—customers. If the team is doing well, it's great for your business to be associated with them.

Look Outside Your Industry

Many of us get so absorbed with our own markets—and the businesses we are competing against—that we judge our performance only against them. But the truth is your customers are comparing your product or service against their experience in other industries too. So make sure you look beyond your own immediate competitors and search for best practice in all fields.

There are some things that are specific to your market, but many aspects of customer service apply across a wide range of sectors. So, whether you are comparing billing systems or sales ideas, look beyond your current experience in search of improvements.

Make No Assumptions

Often we hold the growth of our businesses back by making assumptions about our customers and what they will buy. This can lead to us missing out on opportunities—and even losing customers.

There are several things you should never assume about the customer:

- ➢ They can't afford it
- ➢ They won't buy it
- ➢ They don't understand the product
- ➢ They won't buy more than one
- ➢ They won't price your competitor
- ➢ They won't like you

Making any of these assumptions could be fatal for your business.

However, assuming any of the opposite is just as bad. Therefore, never assume anything—always make an effort to check. Sometimes all you need to do is ask.

News

When you make your marketing topical, it will attract more attention and interest. So you should always be looking for opportunities to tie your message in with anything going on in the news and with current events.

If you have an opinion or valuable information about something going on in the news, issue a press release to seek publicity.

If you tie in your marketing campaigns around major events like the Olympics or the World Series, people will take more interest.

Often being able to be associate yourself with people that are in the news helps you create greater credibility because it seems less like advertising.

Another way of taking advantage of people's interest in the news is by making your advertising look like a news story—complete with headlines and columns—rather than an ad.

In a newspaper, they will probably require the word "advertisement" to be added at the top of your ad, but if you immediately grab their attention, people will quickly forget they are reading an ad.

You can also get these news stories printed up as "tear sheets" and mail them to people.

Offer Information—Two-Step Marketing

The chances of you making a contact with someone and having them buy right away are pretty slim. Sure, it can happen—but it's much more likely that you'll need to find a way to stay in touch with them so that they can get to know you better. If you keep in touch, they are more likely to remember you when they are ready to buy.

However, they are not likely to buy from you if you keep on trying to sell all the time. Therefore, you need to start out by offering them some valuable free information in exchange for their contact details—that could either be their e-mail or the full mailing address.

The free information you offer will depend on your business, but it could be a:

> Fact sheet

> Report or white paper

> Video or audio

> Regular newsletter

Once you've captured their details, you need to keep in touch regularly, continuing to deliver valuable information that helps establish your expertise and build the relationship. You need to mail regularly and often—whether it's once a day, once a week, or a couple of times a month. It depends on your message and your market. People will forget who you are if you only mail them every couple of months.

Personality

It's crucial to remember that ultimately people prefer to buy from other people rather than from faceless corporations. That can mean that you have to build a strong personal relationship with your customers. But the larger your business gets, the more difficult that is.

The secret is to make sure that your business has personality. You can do that by creating a story of the person behind your business.

For example, you might buy:

- Pancakes from Aunt Jemima

- Angel food cakes from Betty Crocker

- Coffee from Juan Valdez

They might be myths, but even myths are comforting.

It can be good to have a story behind your brand and, whether or not your story is true, people are willing to suspend their disbelief if it suits what they want.

Quantify Customer Value

We're all glad to get new customers, and we do our best to take care of them as much as possible.

But it's important to be aware that some of our customers are more valuable to us than others. It's a good idea to know who your most valuable customers are so that you can put that extra effort into taking care of them.

One way you can identify those that are most valuable is to assign each a rating of, for example, A, B, C, or D, taking into account factors such as:

> Profitability

> Time required to care for them

> Special requests

When you complete this exercise, you'll probably discover that some accounts are demanding a lot of your time but not contributing their share of profitability. You can use this information to make sure you maximize the attention you focus on the most profitable clients.

Having a proper evaluation in place allows you to share this information with everyone on the team so that your approach is consistent throughout.

Raise Your Prices

Many people find it too easy to succumb to the pressure of reducing prices to increase sales. But sometimes, the opposite approach can be more effective. Higher prices can position you as different from the competition and can make people see you as more appealing.

For example, someone buying a car may be happy to pay higher prices for a BMW than for another make because they see it is as more reliable or more desirable.

It's rarely a good idea to compete on price and, the truth is, you may be able to charge more than you think.

Rather than thinking of price, it's better to think in terms of value. If people see value in what you offer, they will pay more. So, if you increase your prices, make sure people feel they are getting extra value.

Simplify Lives

Everybody wants their life to be easier, and many are willing to pay premium prices for the privilege. Often being able to simplify someone's life is more important to them than the price.

You can probably think of many products and services that command premium prices because they make life easier, such as:

> ➢ Ready-made sandwiches

> ➢ Cheese slices

> ➢ Microwave meals

> ➢ Dry cleaning delivered

> ➢ Valet parking

Some of these ideas—and many like them—may have seemed crazy at first. But people get used to convenience. If your product or service saves time or makes life easier, they may be ready to pay more.

Telephone

With the growing power of the Internet and so many people getting overloaded with e-mail, some of the traditional methods of communication have actually become more powerful.

The good old telephone can actually work wonders for your business. If you have a new product or marketing idea, why not call a few people up and ask them what they think before you invest too much time and money in developing it.

When you have something to sell, get on the phone—respecting the "do not call" rules, of course. You'll find the response and effectiveness of phone calls could be ten times better than the same number of pieces of mail. And the big advantage is that the feedback you get is faster, better, and more detailed.

Upgrade Customers

Once you have acquired a customer, you want to deepen and lengthen the relationship as much as possible. That means you have to find ways to provide valuable extra services and benefits that make people ready to pay you more.

By enabling people to upgrade to higher levels of service, you are changing the way they see you.

There are many ways you can add value to what you deliver, ranging from regular information and updates to personal consultations and live events.

Upgraded services can move people's perception of you from being just another supplier to being a highly valued expert adviser.

View Your Audience as Individuals

When you are communicating with people in your audience—whether they are customers or prospects—think of them as individuals. When you write to a sea of thousands of anonymous people, your message comes over as very impersonal. You'll get much better results from your ads, brochures, and e-mails when you imagine that you are writing to one individual.

Picture an existing customer or a friend or family member, and then write as if you were having a relaxed conversation with that person. You'll find the message comes over more effectively and the results are much better.

Winners

In any area of life, when you want to achieve great results, it's a good idea to look for people who are already achieving what you want, and then learn from them. So, when you want to improve your marketing, look for companies that you admire and identify what it is about them and their marketing strategies that seem particularly effective.

You don't need to copy them, and no one business has all the answers. Learn from as many as you can, adapt that information to suit your needs, and then continue to improve on them.

You should always be building a "swipe" file—samples of ads, mailing packs, and brochures that you like. You can refer to them when you are looking for ideas or inspiration. Don't copy them exactly, but note whatever you feel makes them effective and think about how that could be applied to your own needs.

Exceed Expectations

The best way to keep your customers happy is to give them more than they expected. You can do that by throwing in a bonus, such as a special report or by doing extra—for example, giving them 125 marketing tips instead of the 100 you promised.

You can often add in little extras that make a big difference to the customer but have little or no cost to you.

You have to go beyond the normal to get noticed. People expect you to do what they pay you for, and they expect you to do it well. To stand out, you have to surprise them and be truly exceptional.

Bear in mind that you have to offer service that you can maintain. If you try to be all things to all people, you will disappoint some.

You don't want to be giving too much away—it needs to be something you can keep doing consistently and profitably.

If you build unreasonable expectations, you will end up disappointing people. So it's important to seek to excel in a way that you will be able to keep up in the future.

YOU - The Industry Expert

The big key to the success of establishing yourself as an industry expert and becoming a local celebrity is—of course—YOU. So you need to be undertaking a range of activities that build your position and that of your business as expert in your field.

One great way to do this is running seminars. These:

> Establish your company as an expert on the subject

> Help cement relationships with customers and prospects

> Increase awareness of your company

Another powerful way of building your brand is writing expert articles—

or even a regular column—for local magazines and newspapers.

These days, a popular way of establishing your expert status is by writing a blog focused on a topic that has broad appeal among your clients and prospect base. A big advantage of blogs is that they act as a channel of two-way communication, and you should encourage people to give you feedback and comments. This helps make you aware of what people think and establishes valuable relationships.

Zero Competition

You want your business to stand out from the competition as much as possible. You can do that through the product or service you offer and the way you position it.

But it's also important to choose your market carefully. Sometimes that means you should leave the most obvious markets to everyone else and find a smaller market or niche that nobody is serving.

When you match the right offer and positioning to the right target market, you are well on the way to success.

Tracy Myers is a car dealership owner, author, speaker and entrepreneur. He recently celebrated the opening of his newest business, The Celebrity Academy in Charlotte, NC. The Academy teaches professionals, entrepreneurs and business owners how to get noticed, gain instant credibility, make millions and dominate their competition by building their expert status.

Following these principles have helped Tracy gain enormous success at his own dealership, Frank Myers Auto Maxx. It was recently recognized as the Number One Small Businesses in NC by Business Leader Magazine, one of the top three dealerships to work for in the country by The Dealer Business Journal, and one of the Top 22 Independent Automotive Retailers in the United States by Auto Dealer Monthly Magazine.

He graduated from the Certified Master Dealer program at Northwood University and was the youngest person to receive the National Quality Dealer Of The Year award, which is the highest obtainable honor in the used car industry.

He has provided guest commentary on the FOX Business Network and has also been featured on NBC, ABC, CBS & FOX affiliates across the country. He has also appeared on stages from coast to coast and is the author of several books, including the #1 best-sellers Uncle Frank Sez, Pushing To The Front (written with the legendary Brian Tracy) and YOU Are The Brand, Stupid!

Tracy and his wife Lorna have made their home in Lewisville, NC with their 2 children Maddie and Presley. He is a Christian Business Owner whose goal is to run his business "By the Book".

Read more about Tracy at TracyMyers.com

Tracy Myers is a car dealership owner, author, speaker and entrepreneur. He recently celebrated the opening of his newest business, The Celebrity Academy in Charlotte, NC. The Academy teaches professionals, entrepreneurs and business owners how to get noticed, gain instant credibility, make millions and dominate their competition by building their expert status.

Following these principles have helped Tracy gain enormous success at his own dealership, Frank Myers Auto Maxx. It was recently recognized as the Number One Small Businesses in NC by Business Leader Magazine, one of the top three dealerships to work for in the country by The Dealer Business Journal, and one of the Top 22 Independent Automotive Retailers in the United States by Auto Dealer Monthly Magazine.

He graduated from the Certified Master Dealer program at Northwood University and was the youngest person to receive the National Quality Dealer Of The Year award, which is the highest obtainable honor in the used car industry.

He has provided guest commentary on the FOX Business Network and has also been featured on NBC, ABC, CBS & FOX affiliates across the country. He has also appeared on stages from coast to coast and is the author of several books, including the #1 best -sellers Uncle Frank Sez, Pushing To The Front (written with the legendary Brian Tracy) and YOU Are The Brand, Stupid!

Tracy and his wife Lorna have made their home in Lewisville, NC with their 2 children Maddie and Presley. He is a Christian Business Owner whose goal is to run his business "By the Book".

Read more about Tracy at TracyMyers.com

CPSIA information can be obtained at www.ICGtesting.com
Printed in the USA
BVOW032117220812

298490BV00002B/1/P